IN HOLLAND STANDS A HOUSE

a play about the life and times of Anne Frank

SUE SAUNDERS

Resource Material
Cecily O'Neill and Sue Saunders

Series Consultant
Cecily O'Neill

Published by CollinsEducational, 77 Fulham Palace Road,
Hammersmith, London W6 8JB

First published 1991

ISBN 0 00 330242 3

Acknowledgements

The following permissions to reproduce material are gratefully
acknowledged:

Text extracts: from *The Diary of Anne Frank* (for the original play) Anne
Frank Fonds; (for the play) Albert Hackett and The Estate of Frances
Goodrich Hackett; from *Anne Frank's Tales of the Secret Annexe*,
Penguin Books Ltd (translated by Ralph Manheim and Michael Mok,
Viking 1985, tranlation © Otto Frank, 1952, 1959, © Doubleday and
Co Inc 1983), and Anne Frank Fonds (performance rights); from *Anne
Frank Remembered*, Transworld Publishers Ltd, © Miep Gies with
Alison Leslie Gold, 1987, published by Bantam Press), and Meredith
Bernstein (performance rights); 'Colours', by Yevgeny Yevtushenko,
Penguin Books Ltd, from *Yevtushenko: Selected Poems*, translated by
Robin Milner-Gulland and Peter Levi, SJ, Penguin Books, 1962
(including performance rights); 'Fear', Penguin Books Ltd, from *Anne
Frank's Tales from the Secret Annexe*, (translated by Ralph Manheim
and Michael Mok, Viking, 1985, translation © Otto Frank, 1952, 1959,
© Doubleday and Co Inc 1983); 'Mending Wall', by Robert Frost,
Jonathan Cape, by permission of the Estate of Robert Frost, from *The
Poetry of Robert Frost*, edited by Edward Connery Lathem; 'Number
One of Twelve Songs', by WH Auden, Faber and Faber, from *Collected
Shorter Poems 1927–1957* by WH Auden, and © WH Auden, 1966,
permission granted by Curtis Brown Ltd, London (performance rights);
'Anne Frank Huis', Andrew Motion; '1945' by Geoffrey Summerfield,
Andre Deutsch Ltd, from *Welcome*.

Music: for 'Refugee Blues', Lucy Rogers.

Illustrations: The Anne Frank Foundation, pages viii, 60, 64, 69 and 71;
The Imperial War Museum, pages ix, and x; Camera Press, pages vi, 67
and 78. *Cover:* Topham Picture Library and The Hulton Picture
Company.

Typeset in Linotron Century Schoolbook by
Northern Phototypesetting Co., Ltd., Bolton
Printed and bound in Great Britain
by Bell & Bain, Thornliebank, Glasgow

CONTENTS

PREFACE

In Holland Stands a House is adapted from Anne Frank's *Diary*
and *Anne Frank's Tales from the Secret Annexe*, also from *Anne
Frank Remembered* by Miep Gies. The play was originally
performed at the Central Newcastle High School (G.P.D.S.T.) in
1987. It runs for approximately one and a half hours.

The adaptor freely acknowledges the inspiration and advice of
the pupils who took part in the original production, together
with those who corresponded with resistance workers in Holland
– Chaim Natkiel, Lex van Weren and Jac van de Kar.

The play is intended to stand as a warning. The idea for
compiling it began for me at the river at Durham, when some
Chinese friends were menaced from the towpath by two British
youths bearing a rock. I was reminded of some lines from Robert
Frost's poem 'Mending Wall':

> '. . . I see him there
> Bringing a stone grasped firmly by the top
> In each hand, like an old-stone savage armed.'

Robert Frost's neighbour claims that the wall is necessary,
even though it serves no practical purpose, and insists that
'Good fences made good neighbours'.

I have used these words to open the play. Whenever we build
barriers between people we risk introducing mistrust,
intolerance and prejudice. We begin a process which can lead, if
it is not checked, to the extremes of racism and fascism. This is
not an easy message. Even Anne herself can be guilty of
intolerance.

S.M.S.

USING THE BOOK

It is possible to use the play text and the accompanying resource material in a number of different ways. Here are some of the possibilities.

- Read the text of *In Holland Stands a House.*
  Use the background information and the resource material as starting points for class discussion or writing assignments, or as stimulus material and ideas for work in drama. This work could be linked with the study of intolerance, racism and fascism, in the past and in society today.
- Work towards a classroom performance of the play.
  Build in ideas and scenes arising from your work on the resource material. Share some of your work informally with other classes, or in school assembly.
- Use your classroom performance as the basis for a more ambitious production involving an extended cast and drawing on resources from the music and art departments.
- Set up an exhibition of background information and pictures as well as writing and art work which have arisen as a result of your work on the play.

From time to time, as you read the play, you will come across one of these: $\boxed{p.\,56}$

Each arrow will direct you to a section of the resource material which relates to the scene you are reading. There you will find suggestions for adding to the play at the point where you meet the arrow.

BACKGROUND TO THE PLAY

After their defeat in the First World War, which was a great
blow to their national pride, the German people faced increasing
economic and social problems. There were huge debts overseas,
and growing poverty and discontent at home. Severe economic
depression caused widespread inflation and unemployment.

Adolf Hitler, the leader of the German National Socialist
Workers' Party, exploited people's fear and discontent. He
blamed the country's problems on his opponents, the
Communists, and above all, on the Jews, who were made the
nation's scapegoats. His party, which became known as the
Nazis, glorified the 'Aryan' or German race, and persecuted
those who were considered racially 'inferior'.

Hitler in 1933

In 1933, the Nazi party won power in the elections and Hitler became Chancellor. Soon he seized absolute power. All trade unions and political parties were forbidden, and the outright persecution of his opponents began. Thousands of Communists and Socialists were arrested and imprisoned in concentration camps.

The Nazis set about achieving their aim of a 'racially pure' German nation. Physically and mentally handicapped people, homosexuals, gypsies, blacks, and above all Jews, were regarded as unfit to be citizens. 'Aryans' – those regarded as pure-blooded Germans – were forbidden to marry Jews. There was forced sterilization for the handicapped and those with disorders like epilepsy, as well as a programme of 'euthanasia', which was the 'legalised' killing of groups which did not fit in with Hitler's image of the new Germany.

Education and leisure activities for young people were tightly controlled. The Hitler Youth was the only youth movement allowed. For boys, the emphasis was on military training, for girls, on preparations for motherhood and domestic life. The Nazis depended on constant propaganda to get across their ideology. Hatred of the Jews was a constant theme. Hitler, aided by his Minister of Propaganda, whipped up fear and hatred against the Jews in his speeches at mass rallies. Soon, the police, the legal system and the army were completely under Hitler's control, and the Jewish population, increasingly isolated, insulted and oppressed, was at the mercy of the Nazis.

Laws were passed which gradually made it impossible for Jewish citizens to live or work in Germany. Jewish shopkeepers, lawyers and doctors were boycotted. Jews were forbidden to own businesses, civil servants with at least one Jewish grandparent lost their jobs, and Jewish children were not allowed to go to the same schools as 'Aryan' children, or to attend universities. Realising that soon even their lives would be threatened, thousands of Jews fled from Germany.

For those who remained behind and for Jews throughout Europe, the situation grew increasingly desperate. In 1938, the first mass arrests of Jews took place. Thousands were rounded up and sent to concentration camps. By 1942, plans were in place to annihilate eleven million European Jews. This genocide, the attempt to exterminate an entire race, was known as 'The Final Solution'. From all over occupied Europe, cattle trucks carried tens of thousands of Jews to their deaths in slave labour camps and the gas chambers of Auschwitz, Dachau, Bergen-Belsen, Buchenwald and many other concentration camps. By the end of the war, six million Jews were dead.

ANNE FRANK

Anne Frank was born on 12 June 1929, in the German city of Frankfurt. Her parents, Otto and Edith Frank, came from well-to-do Jewish families, and had one other child, Margot, who was three years older than Anne.

Otto Frank, Anne's father, was among those who quickly realised that life for Jews would be impossible in Hitler's

The Frank family in 1940

Germany. In 1933 he brought his family to live in Amsterdam. There was a large Jewish community in the city, many of whom were also refugees from the Nazis. Anne and Margot went to local schools, made many friends and quickly learned to speak Dutch. Mr Frank's business prospered, and he took Mr van Daan into the firm. But this peaceful life was not to last.

Hitler's troops invaded Austria and Czechoslovakia, and then, in September 1939, they marched into Poland. Britain and France declared war on Germany on 3 September 1939. The following year, the German army invaded first Denmark and Norway, and then, in May 1940, Holland, Belgium, Luxembourg and France.

The German invasion came as a complete surprise to the Dutch. They had hoped that their country could remain neutral, as it had done in the First World War. The occupation happened

swiftly. After the destruction of the port of Rotterdam by
German bombs, the Dutch had no choice but to surrender. Soon,
anti-Jewish measures were introduced throughout Holland.
Many areas and public facilities were labelled 'Forbidden for
Jews'. Every Jew was required to wear a yellow Star of David,
with the word 'Jew' on it in black letters. Jews were rounded up
without warning in the streets and many disappeared.

Like many others who foresaw that mass arrests and
deportations would soon follow, Otto Frank made plans to
protect his family. He transferred his firm to the control of his
business manager, and began to prepare a hiding-place for his
family and the van Daans in the secret annexe behind his office
and warehouse. In July 1942, Margot, like thousands of other
young Jewish people, received a letter requiring her to report for
transport to a 'work camp' in Germany on the following day.
This was the signal which her parents had been waiting for.
Very early the next day, 6 July, the Frank family moved into the
annexe. A week later, Mr van Daan, his wife and son, Peter, also
moved into the annexe. Later, Mr Dussel joined them.

The eight people in the annexe were totally dependent on their
four helpers: Miep Gies, her husband, and Otto Frank's
employees, Mr Kraler and Mr Koophuis. These four people had
to provide all the food, clothing, medicine, books and other daily
necessities without being noticed by the neighbours or the other
workers in the office and warehouse. The task was made more
difficult by the increasing scarcity of food and other goods in
occupied Holland, particularly in the last years of the war. If
they had been discovered helping those in hiding, these brave
people ran the risk of execution or deportation to the

*A Dutch citizen is rounded up to be transported
to a slave labour camp in Germany*

concentration camps themselves. Both those in hiding and their helpers lived in constant fear of discovery.

For twenty-five months, Anne, the youngest of the eight people in the secret annexe, kept a diary. In it she wrote about the daily life of the annexe, and also about her own growth from an immature schoolgirl into a sensitive adolescent trying to come to terms with life under intensely difficult conditions:

> I want to be out there so much that whenever anyone comes in from the outside with the wind in their clothes and the cold on their faces I could bury my head in the blankets to stop myself longing.

The liberation of Western Europe by the Allied forces began on D-Day, 6 June 1944. That summer, the Dutch were full of hope that the allied armies were approaching. But on 4 August an anonymous telephone call to the police betrayed the hiding-place in the secret annexe. The eight inhabitants, along with Kraler and Koophuis, who were arrested for helping them, were taken away for interrogation. Kraler and Koophuis were sent to work camps, but survived. The others went first to Westerbork,

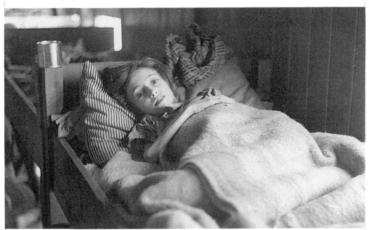

A girl suffering from typhus in Belsen concentration camp

the Dutch transit camp for Jews. They were deported on 3 September, on the last train to leave for Auschwitz, the death camp in Poland. Mrs Frank died in Auschwitz, but Margot and Anne were transferred to Bergen-Belsen, a concentration camp in Germany. There, weakened by hunger and grief, first Margot and then Anne died of typhus. Anne was fifteen when she died in March 1945, three weeks before the camp was liberated by the British. Otto Frank was the only survivor from the secret annexe. Miep Gies, their faithful friend, had managed to save Anne's papers and the books that contained her diary. They were Mr Frank's last link with his family.

Anne's diary was first published in 1947. It is probably the best known book to have been written during the war, and is one of the most widely-read books in the world. Through these pages, Anne speaks directly to us of youth and hope and courage, in spite of the inhuman system under which she suffered and which eventually destroyed her and everything she held dear. Her spirit lives on, and her courage and humanity have made her an inspiration to thousands of people around the world.

The house where Anne and the others lived in hiding is now a museum and education centre, run by the Anne Frank Foundation, which was founded in 1947. Apart from the preservation of the annexe, the Foundation works against anti-semitism, racism and fascism throughout the world, by providing information, educational projects and exhibitions.

FLOOR PLAN OF THE ANNEXE

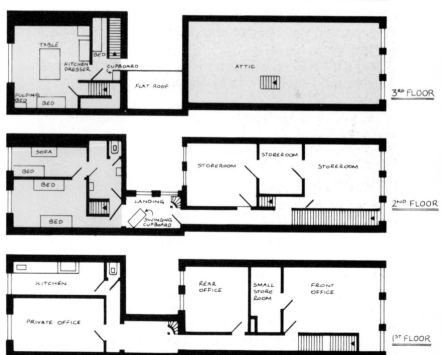

The shaded area shows the space occupied by the Frank family, the van Daans and Mr Dussel.

THE CHARACTERS

CONTROLLER 1 ⎱ both Controllers are strident,
CONTROLLER 2 ⎰ confident and aggressive

CHORUS all shapes, sizes and personalities – they are divided into two groups, who wear Stars of David or Swastikas and are indicated by D1, D2, S1, S2 etc. in the playscript

MIEP GIES *pronounced Meep Gees* in her early twenties, good-natured, self-possessed and courageous

ANNE FRANK in her early teens, attractive, lively, self-willed and idealistic

MARGOT FRANK in her mid-teens, quiet, hard-working and sweet-natured

EDITH FRANK their mother, a gentle woman, trying hard to understand her younger daughter and be the peacemaker

OTTO FRANK their father, a man of integrity and imagination – there is a special bond between him and Anne

MRS VAN DAAN pretty, vain and sometimes rather selfish

MR VAN DAAN rather withdrawn – at times he finds his wife's behaviour trying

PETER VAN DAAN their son, in his mid-teens, shy, sensitive and somewhat immature

ALBERT DUSSEL a dentist, a man of some charm – he can be rather petty

There are also two animal characters whose presence in the play must be imagined:

MOORTIE *pronounced More-tsche* Anne's cat

MOUSCHI *pronounced Moo-shee* Peter's cat

IN HOLLAND STANDS A HOUSE

This introductory sequence describes what happened in the first production of the play. You may wish to begin your production in a different way, depending on the type of performance space you have to work in.

If you are reading the play in class, it may be best to begin at Scene One, page 3.

There are a number of other moments which you will want to omit if you are reading the play in class. These are boxed off from the rest of the playscript, like this.

PROLOGUE

The rostrum, coffee table, and the more elegant chairs and stools are already on stage (see Staging the Play, *page 51). The house lights are still on. Lively, rather off-beat music, reminiscent of a circus, plays.*

The entire cast enters at various points. **Mr** *and* **Mrs Frank, Anne** *and* **Margot** *move the display boards (see* Staging the Play, *page 51). Props are put amongst the audience: the basket of presents by* **Miep,** *the menorah by* **Mr** *and* **Mrs van Daan.** *(These are used in Scene Eleven.)* **Mr Dussell** *and* **Peter** *move in the annexe table, chairs and stools, and stack them in readiness stage right.*

Swastikas and armbands bearing Stars of David are brought in. They are carried in a top hat by the character who plays the photographer (who will later wear a Star of David). The rest of the **Chorus** *crowds round the photographer, talking noisily, and are each given the appropriate emblem, which they help each other to put on. They and the* **Controllers** *wear masks.*

1

The **Controllers** direct operations and organise the **Chorus** into straight lines, Stars of David in one line and Swastikas in another.

The **Frank family** stand on the rostrum. The other named characters go to their starting points (stage left, stage right or in the back area).

When all are ready, the **Controllers** call for the music to be switched off.

CONTROLLER 1 *as if teaching a lesson* Good fences make good neighbours.

The members of the **Chorus** have to be taught this line laboriously. They obviously have no idea what it means. The two **Controllers** share their disgust at these slow learners with the audience. Finally, the **Chorus** is word perfect and very complacent, although they clearly still have no real conception of what the line means.

The **Controllers** call for the house lights to go down, and Scene One begins immediately.

ACT I

SCENE ONE

---

*Slides are projected to illustrate the words of the **Chorus**.*

CONTROLLER 1   1929.

S1   The German city of Frankfurt had a population of 500,000.

D1   30,000 were of the Jewish faith . . .

S2   . . . not to mention the sundry gypsies, blacks, homosexuals, mentally handicapped, physically handicapped and alcoholics . . .

S3   . . . none of them pure white Germans.

D2   In Frankfurt in Germany in 1929, a Jewish couple, Edith and Otto Frank, gave birth to a little girl, Anne . . .

D3   . . . she was their second child.

S4   The Great Depression was upon Germany . . .

S5   . . . 10,000 in the city were unemployed . . .

D4   . . . . and people began to blame the Jews.

S6   Mr Frank had a job.

D5   He had also fought for Germany in the First World War . . .

D6   . . . as did a young soldier called . . .

ALL   Adolf Hitler.

S7   Hitler was a member of the National Socialist German Workers' Party – a Nazi . . .

S8   . . . and on March 23rd, 1933, he seized absolute power in Germany.

D7   All other political parties were forbidden, all political opponents were eliminated.

D8   Jewish doctors were boycotted, Jewish public servants were fired.

S9   *staccato*   No Jew may own his own business.

D9   Mr and Mrs Frank left Germany, and with their daughters – Margot, aged seven, and Anne, aged five – they settled in Amsterdam, in the Netherlands.

Improvisation: the family photograph
To introduce the actors playing the members of the **Frank**
family *to the audience, the photographer moves the family into*
position, addressing each of them clearly by name; he then 'takes'
a studio portrait. As soon as this has happened, a photograph of
the actors, taken earlier, is projected. Throughout this, some
sentimental Germanic folk melody can be played.

CONTROLLER 2   Twelve years later, by the end of the
Second World War, Mr Frank was the only survivor in his
family; six million other European Jews perished, as well as
his wife and daughters. Anne's only legacy was a diary.

End of projection sequence.

SCENE TWO

Swastikas *form circle, stage right;* **Stars of David** *form circle,*
stage left. **Miep** *enters acting area and* **Anne** *runs forward to*
hold her hand.

MIEP   *to audience*   My name is Miep, Miep Gies. Like Anne, I
was German by birth – although I am a Christian. I was sent
to Holland and adopted by a Dutch family because there were
food shortages back home. I soon thought of the Dutch family
as **my** family. When I started work, I was lucky enough to get
a job as an office worker for the firm of Travies and Co which
was owned by a Mr Otto Frank. It wasn't long before I met his
daughter Anne – a little girl with shining, alert eyes – quite a
personality . . .

ANNE   *mimicking her schoolmistress*   As a punishment for
talking, Anne will do a composition entitled ' "Quack, quack,
quack!" says Mrs Natterbeak'.

4

SCENE THREE

Slides of war-torn Europe accompany this scene. **Swastikas** *and* **Stars of David** *march on the spot to the beat of a drum.* **Anne** *runs back to join the family group.*

CONTROLLER 1   In the March of 1939, Czechoslovakia was occupied by Hitler. On September 1st, Hitler's army marched into Poland.

CONTROLLER 2   On September 3rd, England and France declared war on Germany. Holland sat right in the middle of these three countries.

CONTROLLER 1   On November 30th, the Soviet Red Army attacked Finland. But as the Dutch people greeted the New Year and the new decade, the radio was strangely quiet.

CONTROLLER 2   The spring of 1940 burst upon them; the silky air and the lengthening days gave them all feelings of hope for the situation in Europe.

CONTROLLER 1   Perhaps, just perhaps . . .

Sound effect of droning aircraft over the next four speeches.

MIEP   Deep in the night, interrupting my heavy sleep, I heard what sounded like a persistent humming noise, mixed with a faraway muted sound of thunder. Downstairs, someone was turning the static-filled dial of the radio: reports were confusing. Were those German aeroplanes?

ANNE   Dawn broke – the confusion continued. Word came that German soldiers, dressed in Dutch uniforms, were parachuting out of aeroplanes. Also, that guns and bicycles were coming down from the sky.

MIEP   Finally, Queen Wilhelmina spoke on the radio and told us, her voice heavy with emotion, that the Germans had attacked our beloved Holland. It was Friday, May 10th, 1940.

MARGOT   On the evening of May 14th, General Wilkelman came on the radio and announced that the Germans had obliterated Rotterdam with bombs dropped from the air, that floods were spreading across sections of Holland with opened

5

dykes, and that the Germans had threatened to bomb Utrecht and Amsterdam if we continued to resist. In order to spare further loss of life and property, we were surrendering to the Germans.

MRS FRANK   We began to see German uniforms here and there in the street. The German army paraded through Amsterdam, looking triumphant in uniforms and helmets. From out of their rat holes appeared Dutch Nazis, who were cheering and waving and welcoming.

S Chorus arranges the table and chairs stacked stage right to represent an outdoor café.

MR FRANK   But near-normality continued in Amsterdam as summer came. The Germans were trying to win us over with niceness, although the official radio now played nothing but German music and the cinemas showed only German films. It was almost as though nothing had changed until, in an open café, one's eye might light on a Nazi wearing a uniform, or a German policeman – one of those known as the Green Police.

Mr Frank withdraws to the back area, Mrs Frank and Miep to stage left. Anne and Margot sit at the coffee table.

Meanwhile, the D Chorus takes up positions as Dutch citizens enjoying an evening out: couples strolling, children playing. A waltz plays; the Ds dance. During the waltz, taking over from it, come the strains of German military music. Ss move forward menacingly. The Ds hesitate, stop and eventually scatter through the audience to the backstage area, followed by the Ss.

MIEP   It started insidiously, but as the long, dark winter settled over us, the noose around the Jewish neck began to tighten. And my life was also affected, and that of my friends, as I realised one afternoon when the Franks invited me to their house – a social visit that turned out to have far-reaching consequences.

SCENE FOUR

A domestic clock chimes four. Lights come up on stage left, where **Margot** *and* **Anne** *are already seated,* **Anne** *writing her diary and* **Margot** *reading a book.* **Mrs Frank** *brings* **Miep** *forward.*

MRS FRANK   Anne, Margot: Miep has arrived. Anne, chat to her, will you? Margot, help me with the coffee; Daddy will be home soon, with the van Daans and Dussel.

They withdraw stage right.

MIEP   Hello, Anne. It's good to be here again – it always feels so comfortable in your house. Henk and I are still looking for somewhere to settle. It's so hard these days – so many refugees have had to come to Amsterdam – so much overcrowding!

ANNE   Who's Henk?

MIEP   My boyfriend. My fiancé actually! What are you writing?

ANNE   It's my diary, but I'm pretending it's to a friend. I call her Kitty.

MIEP   Why not an ordinary diary – or a real friend?

ANNE   I don't want to set down a series of bald facts in a diary like most people do. Anyway, I don't know anyone I can really talk to.

MARGOT   *coming forward with a tray and cups*   Anne, how can you say that! Don't listen to her, Miep. She's the most popular girl in school and she can wind us all round her little finger! And does, frequently!

Margot *withdraws during the next speech.*

ANNE   Well, I know I've got parents, *sarcastically*   and a big sister of 16. I know about thirty people you might call friends – I have strings of boyfriends! Don't laugh! I can't seem to avoid it at our school. As soon as a boy asks if he may cycle home with me and we get into conversation, nine times out of ten I can be sure that he will fall head over heels in love immediately and simply won't allow me out of his sight.   *She acts out this scene.*   If he starts wanting to know when he can have tea at my place, I swerve slightly, my satchel falls, he gets off his bike to hand it to me, by which time I've introduced a new topic of conversation! But it's the same

7

with all my friends, just fun and games, nothing more; I can never bring myself to talk about anything that really matters. We don't seem to be able to get any closer. Perhaps I really lack confidence, in spite of what Margot says. I have a nicer, quieter side. So this diary. *Importantly, as if quoting* Paper is more patient than man! But I'll call it Kitty anyway, whatever anyone says, until I'm older and then I suppose with any luck I'll have a husband like Henk to confide in.

MIEP I hope you will. I love him very much.

ANNE If you love him, why do you look so sad?

Mrs Frank and Margot come forward with the coffee.

MRS FRANK Anne, really!

MIEP No, Mrs Frank, I don't mind, really! *To Anne* It's just that . . . I don't know how I shall ever be able to marry him. I'm not a Dutch citizen, you see – I'm really German.

ANNE Like us?

MIEP Yes, from Vienna. I was very sickly as a child – can you believe that? As skinny as you were when I first knew you, with your socks round your ankles – oh yes! Do you remember, Mrs Frank?

MRS FRANK I certainly do!

MIEP My parents sent me to Holland to fatten up, and here I've stayed.

Mr Frank comes forward from the back area with Mr Dussel and Mr and Mrs van Daan.

DUSSEL Just like me, Miep.

MRS FRANK Miep, you know Mr Dussel, the dentist, don't you?

MIEP Of course I do. He still treats me.

DUSSEL Though she shouldn't be giving me her custom, should you, Miep? A good Christian girl should abandon her bad Jewish dentist. Toothache or no.

MIEP When my Jewish dentist looks like Maurice Chevalier, why should I change!

ANNE *aside to Margot* I thought Miep had good taste! Does he look like Maurice Chevalier?

MARGOT Anne, shut up.

Mr and Mrs van Daan step forward.

MR FRANK Anne, Margot – meet my partner, Mr van Daan,

8

and his wife.

MRS VAN DAAN   Hello!

MRS FRANK   Sit down everyone. Miep was telling us of her problem as you came in there. Go on, Miep.

Coffee is served. **Anne** *and* **Margot** *sit on the floor.* **Anne** *strokes her cat.*

MIEP   Where was I? Oh yes, I'm not a Dutch citizen. A few months ago I was sent for by the German consulate – they invalidated my passport – a big black X on the third page.

MARGOT   Why?

MIEP   Do you remember, Mr Frank, two years ago, that awful little know-all Miss Heep, who worked in the office with me for a few months? She wanted me to join the National Socialist Party.

ANNE   The Nazis!

MIEP   I refused, and it was obviously noted.

ANNE   The little sneak!

MIEP   Well, be that as it may, it's finished me. I have to go back to Germany unless I get married, and I can't get married without my birth certificate, and my uncle in Germany can't send it without my passport, and once they see the X in the passport, the authorities there will refuse to post my birth certificate on. I'm well and truly stuck!

MARGOT   Can't anything be done?

MR FRANK   Wait a minute. What if you had a photograph made of the first page – without the X – and sent that to Germany? Just tell them that you imagine it's proof enough and that you can't be expected to walk around here with no passport or you'll be arrested. It might work.

MIEP   That's brilliant!

ANNE   I have a very intelligent father, haven't I, Pim? Now Miep will marry Henk and they'll live happily ever after.

MRS VAN DAAN   That's more than the rest of us can hope for!

ANNE   Can we go to the wedding, Pim? I'll wear my princess-style coat and my matching cloche hat with a ribbon. *To her cat* I'll look like a real film-star then, won't I, Moortie?

DUSSEL   And what about those of us with Aryan – Christian – wives? My Lotte came here with me from Germany – to what? Deportation and death.

MR VAN DAAN *warningly, with a glance at* **Anne** *and* **Margot** Albert!

MRS FRANK Anne, Margot, clear the coffee cups away will you please? *As* **Anne** *is about to protest* And have another slice of cake in the kitchen!

Anne and **Margot** *clear cups and withdraw stage right.*

MR VAN DAAN Surely you exaggerate!

DUSSEL Look, have you seen the Nazi newspaper? 'Fighting broke out between Jews and Nazis on February 12th here in Amsterdam in the old quarter . . .' This is what it says later: . . . 'Jews ripped open the necks of Nazi soldiers with sharpened teeth and sucked their blood like vampires.' What sort of reprisals are going to follow that sort of poison?

MRS VAN DAAN How many people are burning anti-Nazi newspapers because they're afraid of being found with them? Or English books? Or even dictionaries.

DUSSEL That's not the worst of it. It's wondering about the people who might just have Nazi sympathies – people like Miep's Miss Heep, or people we've known all along who might be spies. And what we might have said to them!

MRS VAN DAAN And we're all registered with the census office, every single Jew in Amsterdam. What does that mean?

MIEP Surely just bureaucratic red tape! After all, I've had to fill in endless forms as well – so's Henk! 'How long have you lived here? What faith? Were your grandparents Dutch? What about great-grandparents?'

MR FRANK In other words, was there a Jew up there somewhere!

MIEP Even if there wasn't it doesn't make me feel any different from you.

MR FRANK Don't you see, Miep, just by telling them, 'I'm an Aryan – a pure white European' you're acknowledging a difference? Don't you understand? Just supposing everyone who fills in those forms refuses to answer either way. What then? Then where would they be?

MR VAN DAAN Fighting a difference that no one acknowledged existed! That's what we need. That's the only thing that can save us now. Everyone sticking to their principles.

MRS FRANK That's asking an awful lot, isn't it? How can we expect ordinary families to guard us as well as struggle through for themselves. I think we're on our own.

MIEP No, Mrs Frank. No, I can't believe that.

Everyone stands up. **Mrs Frank** *moves away with the* **van Daans** *and* **Dussel**, *saying their goodbyes. They go to the back area.*

Look what happened when the decree went out that all Jews should wear a Star of David: that morning there were so many Christians wearing the star that you couldn't possibly have felt on your own.

MR FRANK And now, Miep? Even you wear no star now. Look, your faith in human nature is touching, but do you realise how different we are made to feel? Anne, Margot . . . I feel somehow so guilty at even having brought them into such a world as this.

MIEP Mr Frank, they're happy children! Anne, she doesn't really understand my problem over the marriage; she's just thinking of how romantic it all seems to her!

MR FRANK Do you know what it's like for them, Miep? Think, just think what the occupation has meant to a Jewish child . . .

Miep and Mr Frank withdraw stage right.

SCENE FIVE

Note: The name 'Jopie' is pronounced 'Yo-pee'.

Anne and Margot *stand centre stage. Members of the* **S Chorus** *move up from the back area.*

ANNE Margot, let's go to the park!

MARGOT What time is it?

As the speak, various of the **S Chorus** *move forward between them.*

S3 NO JEW IS TO BE ON THE STREET AFTER 8 O'CLOCK AT NIGHT.

ANNE We've just got time if we go on the bikes.

S4 NO JEW MAY RIDE A BICYCLE. ALL BICYCLES ARE TO BE HANDED IN.

MARGOT We'll go on the tram.

S5 JEWS ARE BANNED FROM PUBLIC TRANSPORT AND MAY NOT DRIVE.

MARGOT We'll walk to the park.

S1 ALL PARKS, TENNIS COURTS, CINEMAS AND OTHER PUBLIC PLACES ARE PROHIBITED TO JEWS.

ANNE Let's listen to the radio.

S6 NO JEW MAY POSSESS A RADIO.

MARGOT Why don't you phone Jopie? She always cheers you up.

S2 NO JEW MAY POSSESS A TELEPHONE.

ANNE Jopie always says you're scared to do anything because it may be forbidden. *Mimics* All Jews are banned from laughing between 9.0 am and midnight!

MARGOT Oh Anne, when will you ever be serious!

ANNE Never – I hope! *She runs off stage right –* **Margot** *follows.*

The **S Chorus** *returns to the back area.*

SCENE SIX

Miep and **Mr Frank** *move forward.*

MIEP I'm sorry. I suppose I was just trying to cheer you up.

MR FRANK I understand that, Miep, but it can't just be pushed aside anymore. We shall have to go into hiding. The van Daans – we've discussed it. They'll join us. If you and Elli are willing there is the annexe above the warehouse and offices.

MIEP Prinsengracht Street is right in the middle of Amsterdam!

MR FRANK Often the most unlikely place is the safest – if you can trust your friends, if you have their support. Miep, it's dangerous. You know what will happen if you're caught! I've had a word with Koophuis and Kraler. The firm's in their name now anyway, thanks to the ban on Jewish-owned businesses. It's terrible to feel so redundant!

MIEP You know we all rely on your wisdom, Mr Frank. You're calmness itself in a crisis, and Heaven knows there's plenty of those, in business and out!

MR FRANK You're avoiding the issue, Miep – the danger if you're caught. It'll mean arrest, probably death. I still have to have your consent, and Elli's; as office workers you're in the front line if the Nazis break in. Koophuis and Kraler may be in charge, but you're every bit as important. Please think.

MIEP I don't need to, Mr Frank. There's no question of not helping you.

MR FRANK We'll make the preparations then, Miep. I daresay the crisis will come of its own accord!

SCENE SEVEN

Note: A 'razzia' (pronounced 'ratz-eea') was the name given to a round-up by the Nazis.

Weird lighting; drum beats and percussion. At the start of the scene the **Chorus** *and* **Controllers** *are in the back area.*

CHORUS *whisper* Razzia! Razzia! Razzia! Razzia!

CONTROLLER 2 *vehemently* Gentlemen, I must ask you to arm yourselves against all feelings of pity. We must destroy the Jews wherever we meet them and whenever possible. Don't think that you can fight a disease without killing the germ, without destroying the bacillus.

CHORUS *quietly* Razzia! Razzia!

CONTROLLER 2 *reasonably* 12,000 or 15,000 Jewish scoundrels eliminated by poison gas in 1914 might perhaps have saved the lives of a million decent Germans.

CHORUS *quietly* Razzia!

CONTROLLER 2 February 1941 – 400 Jewish men and boys were grabbed off the streets, and from houses and coffee shops; beaten and taken away.

CONTROLLER 1 That was the first of the razzias, the round-ups.

CHORUS Razzia . . . *repeated, and rising to a crescendo.*

13

Frantically, the **Ds** *move through the audience, sometimes running backwards to face them and plead with them. The* **Ss** *pursue slowly, relentlessly, coming from all sides and behind.*

D2 Come on, quick!

D10 *to audience* Hide us, please!

D CHORUS Hide us, hide us, hide us, hide us. SAVE US!

There is a sudden silence. The **Ss** *drag* **Ds** *into a semicircle.*

Song by one of the **D Chorus**, *expressing the feeling of abandonment experienced by the refugees; other members of the* **D Chorus** *mime out what is suggested by the words whilst members of the* **S Chorus** *act out the part of those in authority who chose to ignore their plight. (The words and music used in the original production are in the back of the book. See page 65.)*

SCENE EIGHT

During the song Anne has positioned herself with her cat to the right of the table.

ANNE Countless friends and acquaintances have gone. . . . Oh, Moortie, I feel so wicked sleeping in a soft bed, or sitting here, stroking your soft fur . . . and all the while my dearest friends have been knocked down or have fallen into a gutter somewhere out in the cold night.

MARGOT Anne! The SS have sent a call-up notice for Daddy!

ANNE What does that mean? A concentration camp? We can't let Pim be doomed to a lonely cell for the rest of his life!

MARGOT Don't be so melodramatic, Anne! It's more serious than that. Oh, I do wish he'd get home!

ANNE Where is he?

MARGOT He's doing his hospital visiting at the Charity Institute. *Doorbell*

ANNE Don't open the door! *Silence, as they look to the back area.*

MARGOT It's just Mr van Daan!

Margot withdraws stage right to fetch suitcases and some of what is to be put in them.

14

ANNE *She gets up and moves towards stage right.* Margot and I were sent out of the room. Van Daan wanted to talk to Mummy alone. When we were together in our bedroom Margot told me that the call-up notice was not for Daddy but for her. I was more frightened then ever. Margot is sixteen; would they really take girls of that age away alone? But thank goodness she won't go. Mummy said so herself; that must be what Pim meant when he talked about going into hiding. Into hiding . . . where would we go? In a town, or the country – in a house or a cottage?

---

p·56

Improvisation: packing
Margot *encourages* **Anne** *to pack.* **Anne** *brings up the subject of taking her cat.* **Margot** *resists the suggestion and they argue.*

Mr and Mrs Frank and Miep come from the back area. Margot and Miep go for more suitcases and contents throughout the ensuing dialogue.

ANNE Pim, I can take Moortie with me, can't I?

MR FRANK Anne, no . . . I'm sorry! *To Mrs Frank* Why didn't you explain?

MRS FRANK There was no time! How could I have done . . .

MR FRANK All right, all right! It doesn't matter. Anne, our hiding place isn't anywhere strange or different . . . it's going to be on Prinsengracht Street, my office. Miep can help us there. Dear, loyal Miep! You know how she's always been our friend.

ANNE But Pim, if it's your office and we know it, it'll be easier to have Moortie!

MRS FRANK You don't understand, Anne . . . you've got to leave it to us!

ANNE That's what you always say! I'm sick of being treated like a baby.

MARGOT Anne, please!

MR FRANK It's not that, Anne, please believe me! Just trust us a little to know what can and can't be done – right? *Anne nods.* Now, we shan't be able to make any noise in the day at all. We shan't be able to go out . . . yes, I really mean that. Not at all! Now, what sort of life for a cat do you think that is? Yes, I know, it's not much of a life for us either, but at least you and

15

Margot will have your books and your thoughts . . . and us. And company! Mr and Mrs van Daan will be coming too, and their son, Peter . . . we'll all be there together. And we'll win through. Please trust me! Now, we've got to make plans for tomorrow. Margot, I don't like to say it, but the danger's to you first and foremost. You and Miep will go off first, by bicycle.

MRS FRANK What about the Star of David on her coat, Otto? If she's seen riding a bicycle . . .

MR FRANK She'll just have to take it off . . . we've got to take the risk, Edith.

MRS FRANK We're going to follow later, Anne, on foot, with as many clothes as we can wear. Heaven knows how long we'll be there, or how much you'll grow!

ANNE What about the things we'll need in the annexe? Something to cook with, beds, something to sit on . . .?

MRS FRANK We've been collecting things for months now, Anne. Miep, Elli, Kraler, Koophuis: they've all been helping.

MIEP And Henk and I will be back later tonight to take away as much as we can of the stuff you couldn't part with sooner – books, shoes. . . .

MARGOT You're very good to us, Miep.

MIEP It's the least I can do. Without your father I wouldn't be married to Henk; I would have been deported. Right, what can I take with me now? Anne, what about your diary?

ANNE Thanks, Miep, but I'll carry that myself!

Miep, Mr Frank and Margot remove suitcases and withdraw round the side to the back area. Margot, Mr and Mrs Frank don coats; those belonging to Mr and Mrs Frank have Stars of David pinned to them.

ANNE *to audience* Mummy called me at 5.30 and I got dressed – two vests, three pairs of knickers, a dress; on top of that a skirt, jacket, summer coat, two pairs of stockings, lace-up shoes, woolly cap, scarf and still more; I was nearly stifled before we started, but no one inquired about that! Margot rode off behind Miep, into the unknown as far as I was concerned.

Moortie . . .

Improvisation: saying goodbye
Anne *talks to her cat. Ends 'I'll be back, I promise you.' Poignant
music continues through the improvisation, up to the start of
Scene Nine.*

MRS FRANK   *returning to stage area*   Come on, Anne, here
we go!

She helps **Anne** *on with her coat and goes to join* **Margot** *and*
Mr Frank.

ANNE   *to audience*   So we walked in the pouring rain: Daddy,
Mummy and I. We got sympathetic looks from people on their
way to work. You could see from their faces how sorry they
were they couldn't offer us a lift; the gaudy yellow star spoke
for itself. The date is July 9th, 1942.

Anne *picks up her suitcase and moves stage right. At the last
moment she sees her diary on the coffee table, puts down the case
and runs back for it. Then she also goes round the side to the back
area.*

ANNE   *the voice is prerecorded*   I am Anne Frank, aged 14.
This is the last walk I shall ever take freely in the open air . . .

The **Chorus** *moves forward to remove the coffee table with its
stools and chairs. They move the annexe table, chairs and stools
into position, and shift the rostrum.*

17

SCENE NINE

Slides of the house in Prinsengracht Street and of the annexe accompany this scene.

*In the back area stand the **Controllers** and three of the **Ds**, posing as a modern family and two guides showing them round the house.*

*Mr and **Mrs van Daan**, **Peter** and the **Frank family** – still wearing coats and, with the exception of **Margot**, carrying cases – move stage right round the back, through the audience, up the 'staircase' to the annexe, and over to unpack beside the annexe table stage left.*

CONTROLLER 2   Of course, we have to remember that the hiding place was familiar territory to Mr Frank: this had been his place of work. We've just come in through the front door right beside the warehouse, and we're now in the large main office. This is where Elli, Miep, and Mr Koophuis worked.

D4   Who was Mr Koophuis?

CONTROLLER 2   He took over as manager of Mr Frank's spice firm. A little further on, in here, is Kraler's office; he was the partner in the business. And here, up these four steps, is the private office, where the refugees in the annexe could come in the evenings and listen to the radio after the workers had gone home. This was the height of luxury for them.

D9   Did any of the workers know that they were here?

CONTROLLER 2   Just Elli, Miep, Kraler and Koophuis. They had to be absolutely silent during the day, otherwise the warehousemen might have heard them. I'll pass you over to my colleague now. I hope you find the rest of the building interesting!

They move up the staircase and stand stage right of the rostrum.

CONTROLLER 1   This is the annexe itself. A bookcase was built a few weeks after they moved in to conceal the entrance. Mind the stairs – they're very steep!

Westerkirk clock chimes

D4   What's that sound?

CONTROLLER 1   That's the clock from the church tower nearby.

ANNE *at the rostrum* Daddy, Mummy and Margot can't get used to the sound of the clock yet, which tells us of the time every quarter of an hour. I loved it from the start, and especially in the night when it seems like a faithful friend.

CONTROLLER 1 You're standing just outside the Frank family's bedsitting room; on the right is the bathroom and toilet, which they couldn't flush during the day, of course. And here, through the bathroom, is the room Margot and Anne shared; at least until Mr Dussel came.

MR FRANK *at the table* Anne, come here!

ANNE *moving to the table* What is it?

CONTROLLER 1 Anne had a film star collection. You can still see it on the wall here.

D4 Who's this one?

D9 Ginger Rogers, I think.

D3 Is that Princess Margaret as a little girl?

D9 I think it is. There's the Queen too.

ANNE Daddy! You've brought them! Margot, look! Oh, that's wonderful!

She runs back over to **Margot,** *who is now at the rostrum.*

MARGOT Why don't you paste them on the wall?

ANNE Would you mind sharing a room with Clark Gable?

MARGOT Of course not! Look, we can make the wall one gigantic picture. *She coughs.*

ANNE Margot, what would happen to us if someone got very ill in here?

CONTROLLER 1 *moving stage left of the rostrum* And this is the next flight of stairs, leading up to the sitting room and kitchen. Mr and Mrs van Daan slept here also when they arrived.

D3 Didn't they have a son called Peter?

CONTROLLER 1 Yes. He had the little corridor room alongside.

D9 Wasn't there some sort of romance between Anne and Peter?

CONTROLLER 1 Not at first!

ANNE I still don't like Peter any better; he is so boring; he flops lazily on his bed half the time, does a bit of carpentry and then goes back for another snooze. What a fool! He's got a nice cat, though; its called Mouschi. Now that's typical of the van

Daans! Peter has to have his cat; why couldn't I have brought Moortie? But then, Peter's spoilt.

Margot faces stage right. A lighting effect suggests a barred window.

MARGOT   Anne, look! We can get right up to the top attic here. I suppose there won't be any chance of fresh air unless we sit here with the window open.

ANNE   It's lovely, though, isn't it? Look, Margot! There's a chestnut tree – and some seagulls! You can see the birds flying.

D4   Where on earth did Dussel, the dentist, go when he arrived?

Dussel comes up the staircase with coat and suitcase. He looks about him in bewilderment.

CONTROLLER 1   He had to share a room with Anne, and Margot moved in with her parents. Anne didn't like it much! Well, there you are. That's where they all stayed, from July 9th, 1942, until August 4th, 1944.

The Controllers and Ds move off down the staircase.

SCENE TEN

Dussel moves forward to the table as Anne and Margot join the rest.

DUSSEL   I just can't believe how much room there is up here. And I thought you were in Belgium, not in the middle of Amsterdam! I never thought when I asked Miep about a hiding place that you would be here.

MR FRANK   The address in Belgium was the one we left the lodger to find. No, we've been in the annexe all the time, Dussel; for four months now.

DUSSEL   It's incredible!

ANNE   It's like being in a very peculiar sort of boarding house, Mr Dussel.

PETER   We have rules too, Mr Dussel.

ANNE   Oh yes! Just like a boarding house. Let's show him, Peter.

PETER   *mock-seriously*   He'll have to sit down, you know. An honoured guest!

ANNE   Yes! Fetch a chair, Peter. Come on, everyone! The reception committee!

---

*They all bustle around to form a mock-serious reception committee. **Anne** elaborately dusts a chair for **Dussel**. She stands on a stool, **Peter** on the table. 'Hurry' music plays throughout the rest of the scene.*

PETER   Prospectus and Guide to the Secret Annexe. Special institution for Jews and suchlike.

MRS VAN DAAN   Open all the year round. Beautiful, quiet, free from woodland surroundings, in the heart of Amsterdam. Can be reached by trams 13 and 17; also by car and bicycle. In special cases also on foot, if the Germans prevent the use of transport.

PETER   Board and lodging . . .

ALL   Free!

PETER   Special fat-free diet.

MARGOT   Running water in the bathroom . . .

MRS FRANK   . . . Alas, no bath . . .

MARGOT   . . . and down various inside and outside walls.

MR VAN DAAN   Own radio centre: direct communication with London, Tel Aviv, New York and numerous other stations. This appliance is only for residents' use after six o'clock.

MRS FRANK   Rest hours: 10 o'clock in the evening until 7.30 in the morning. 10.15 on Sundays. For reasons of public security, rest hours must be strictly observed!

ANNE   Holidays – postponed indefinitely.

MARGOT   Speak softly at all times – by order! All civilised languages are permitted . . .

ALL   Therefore, no German!

ANNE   Lessons – one written shorthand lesson per week. English, French, Maths and History at all times.

MRS VAN DAAN   Breakfast, every day – 9 am. Sundays and Bank Holidays, 11.30 am.

MRS FRANK   Approximately!

MRS VAN DAAN   Approximately!

MR VAN DAAN   Lunch . . .

PETER . . . Not very big . . .

MR VAN DAAN . . . 1.15 pm to 1.45 pm.

MR FRANK Dinner – cold and/or hot . . .

MR VAN DAAN No fixed time – depends on the news broadcast.

DUSSEL Alcoholic beverages?

ANNE Only with doctor's prescription!

SCENE ELEVEN

p.57

Improvisation: daily life
*The two families and **Dussel** are around the annexe table. From now on, they each have activities that they can be doing in odd moments: reading, knitting, mending, writing. **Anne** writes in her diary.*

The area to the far left and behind the table is the kitchen; perhaps a much smaller table or stool around which there can be a couple of pans and a few other kitchen implements. If working in the kitchen, characters can stand or kneel in this area. There must be an atmosphere of claustrophobia.

*The rostrum, with about four blankets and a suitcase underneath it, represents **Anne's** bedroom.*

The church clock strikes one o'clock.

ANNE Dear Kitty, Dussel is a very nice man, just as we had all imagined. Of course, he thought it was all right to share my little room. Quite honestly I'm not so keen that a stranger should use my things, but one must be prepared . . .

MIEP *Miep comes up the staircase.* Hallo! Where is everyone? I've brought the vegetables and your shorthand homework, Margot! In my name you got everything right!

MRS FRANK What would we do without you! Anne, we'll have a Chanukah feast after all!

MRS VAN DAAN Anne, are you going to help with the potatoes? *to **Mr van Daan*** Honestly, she's frightfully spoilt. I wouldn't put up with it if she were my daughter.

MRS FRANK   Oh, she's always keen to hear Miep's news. The potatoes can wait a little, surely!

MRS VAN DAAN   Come on, Peter. *Peter gets up irritably.*   At least someone always does as he's told!

Mrs van Daan, Peter and Mrs Frank move to the kitchen area.

ANNE   Miep, how's Jopie? You know, my friend who lives in your street. I dreamt the Green Police came and took her away. She was on the train going to Grand Central Station, just like you were telling us was happening.

MR VAN DAAN   Where do they go from there, Miep? Does anyone know?

MIEP   To the holding camp at Westerbork, Mr van Daan, and then on from there. I don't know much more than that.

ANNE   What about Jopie?

MIEP   I think she's still at home, Anne. I've seen Jopie's mother; she still looks the same. Now then, take that through to your mother.   *She hands her some vegetables.*

MARGOT   Are you going to celebrate Christmas this year, Miep, or have any presents on Saint Nicholas' Day?

MIEP   Oh, I think so. I don't suppose you're very interested in Christmas, though!

MARGOT   We have Chanukah at the same time.

MIEP   Chanukah?

MARGOT   It's our festival of light. You see, thousands of years ago, the temple in Jerusalem was destroyed, and when the Jews came back to rebuild it they needed to light the holy candles. But they could only find enough oil to burn for one day, and it was going to take much longer than that to get a fresh supply. Anyway, they started to use the oil and, by a miracle, it lasted the eight days it took to fetch more. That's why we have an eight-branched candlestick at Chanukah. Maybe remembering to light it this year will bring us another miracle!

MIEP   *to audience*   Elli and I began to plan to make a festive Saint Nicholas' Day for the hiding place. Since it was impossible to buy things in the shops we were forced to use lots of ingenuity. We sewed, hammered and glued, and hid the colourful basket of tokens and poems until the evening of December 6th . . .

*The table has been cleared and **Mr van Daan** has fetched the box
containing the menorah from its hiding place in the audience.
Anne fetches the basket of presents hidden by **Miep** at the
beginning of the play.*

p.57

Improvisation: the giving of presents
The presents are distributed. Peter receives a cap.

ANNE   I think Miep and Elli are the best St Nicholases ever!
Are you pleased with your cap, Peter)?   *Looks at him
critically*   It rather suits you!

PETER   What did you get?

ANNE   Oh, this and that! It's a funny thing, though. It's all
much more exciting than it used to be at home. I don't
remember being pleased with presents like I've been with
these – not ever!

PETER   What about when you got your diary?

ANNE   I don't remember telling you about my diary!

PETER   You're always writing in it, so I noticed. And Margot
told me it was your thirteenth birthday present. Oh, don't
worry; I know how to keep a secret.

ANNE   I just hope you do!

MRS FRANK   Has everyone finished? Let's have the candles.
Have you got the menorah, Mr van Daan?

MR VAN DAAN   It's not much, I'm afraid.   *Opening the
box*   Peter made it at school, when he was about eight, I think
. . . *Lighting the candles . . .* there!

DUSSEL   Now, the Chanukah song.

*They all sing. (The words and music are given in the back of the
book. See page 83.)*

SCENE TWELVE

The lighting has dimmed during the song so that the family are seen grouped round the table in the candlelight.

*In the back area the **Chorus** has gathered. It is not relevant at this point which mask they are wearing.*

ANNE   I see the eight of us with our 'Secret Annexe' as if we were a little piece of blue heaven surrounded by heavy black rain clouds. The round, clearly defined spot where we stand is still safe, but the clouds gather more closely about us, and the circle which separates us from the approaching danger closes more and more tightly. Oh, if only the black circle could recede and open the way for us!

D8   Lex van Weren – a musician, inmate of Auschwitz extermination camp . . .

S8   The Germans loved music. Just before Christmas they discovered I could play the trumpet. My life was saved.

D7   Each day the workers at the camp were sent out on the land; on a bowl of soup and a hunk of bread they endured the harshest of labours.

*One of the **Chorus** begins singing 'Silent Night'.*

S9   There was a beautiful Christmas tree in the central square of the camp . . .

D5   At evening the workers returned. Many had not survived the day.

D1   Their bodies were carried in an old cart that trundled its way into the camp and on into the square. . . .

S7   Under the Christmas tree, as the band played 'Silent Night', the bodies were laid out. The tune didn't go too well but it was somehow recognisable.

*The singing of 'Silent Night' is continued as the **Chorus** moves out through the audience. The inhabitants of the annexe also turn and leave. The singing continues in the distance.*

ACT II

SCENE THIRTEEN

RADIO BROADCAST   In the event of a British landing in Holland, the Germans will do all they can to defend the country; if necessary they will resort to flooding. Maps have been published on which the parts of Holland which will be under water are marked. Large sections of Amsterdam are included in this scheme.

Babble of noise from everyone.

MRS VAN DAAN   We'll all drown!

They walk up the staircase to the stage area, and gather round the table.

MR FRANK   Of course not; we'll just have to get out quickly, that's all!

MRS VAN DAAN   *sarcastically*   Fine! Then what would we do with water a metre high? Walk . . . cycle?

ANNE   *flippantly*   We'll have to swim: all put on our bathing suits and caps and swim underwater as much as possible, then no one will see that we are Jews.

DUSSEL   I'd like to see *you* swimming if the rats bit your legs!

ANNE   I wonder who'd scream the loudest?

MRS FRANK   Anne, don't be so rude!

MARGOT   We shan't be able to get out of the house anyway. The warehouse would definitely collapse if there was a flood – it's wobbly already!

MR VAN DAAN Listen! Joking apart, we'd have to find a boat.

ANNE Why bother? I know something much better. We each get hold of a wooden packing case from the attic and row with a soup ladle!

DUSSEL Do you *always* have to sound as though you know best?

MRS FRANK I think Anne was only joking, Mr Dussel!

DUSSEL She spends her whole time joking, except when she's off on a selfish little tack of her own. Do you know what she did today? She asked if I would move out of our room in the afternoon!

ANNE Only twice a week, Mr Dussel: from four o'clock to five thirty. . . . And I didn't ask you to move out. I just asked if I could have the table to work on!

DUSSEL That's not the point . . .

MR FRANK Actually she had my full permission to ask you, politely. I hope it *was* politely, Anne!

MRS VAN DAAN She doesn't know how to be polite!

MRS FRANK That's unfair, Mrs van Daan, she does try!

DUSSEL I have to work, and if I can't work in the afternoons then there's no time left for me at all. If I get interrupted I might as well never have started. Anyway she doesn't work seriously at anything. Greek mythology! What sort of work is that? Knitting and reading – that's not work!

MARGOT Anne *does* work, Mr Dussel. She's really serious about it.

PETER She is, Mr Dussel. She gets me to go through things with her sometimes and I only wish I could be half as self-disciplined. *To Anne* What did you do last week?

ANNE I translated a piece from Dutch into English about Nelson's last battle, read up about coffee growing in Brazil, studied broad and narrow-nosed monkeys, read some of Oscar Wilde's 'An Ideal Husband', in English, mugged up a bit of the Bible, did Charles V . . . What else, Peter?

PETER A comparison of the Mississippi and the Missouri, and some French verbs – I tested her on them.

MRS VAN DAAN *waspishly* So you see there is *someone* who's convinced she's wonderful, Mr Dussel. And the rest of us don't count, of course!

DUSSEL If Margot had asked me I would never have refused.

It's just the way *she* does things: she always assumes that the other person is going to give in.

MR FRANK   Surely you can give her a little time, Albert? She really is making an honest effort to keep up with her education.

DUSSEL   If you wish, yes. But I don't approve. She's an insufferable baby. It's hard to believe that Margot is only two years older than her; Margot's so sensible.

ANNE   *losing her temper*   Why's everything got to be so sensible here? I'm sick of it! Learning to obey, to shut up, to help, to be good, to give in . . . I'll use up all my brains too quickly and I haven't got so many in the first place!   *Anne moves over to the rostrum where she sits with the rug over her, back half-turned.*   I shan't have any left for when the war's over. If I stay here much longer I'll grow up into a dried-up old beanstalk, and I did so want to grow into a *real* young woman!

SCENE FOURTEEN

Mrs Frank moves over to sit on the rostrum.

MRS FRANK   Anne, please don't make such a scene about everything!

ANNE   Me make a scene . . . !

MRS FRANK   Well, you know what I mean! . . . Anne . . . Will you listen to me?

ANNE   Go away!

MRS FRANK   Come on, dear – would you like me to hear your prayers tonight? Daddy can't come just yet . . . Anne! . . . You don't find Margot doing this!

ANNE   I don't in the least want to be like Margot. She lets everyone walk over her and gives in about everything!

MRS FRANK   Very well, then. I don't want to be cross. Love can't be forced, I suppose.   *She turns to go.*

ANNE   I don't care what you think of me.

MRS FRANK   *turning back*   Or what anyone else thinks, I suppose.

ANNE   What's that supposed to mean?

MRS FRANK   I've been wanting to speak to you for a while about . . . well . . . about you and Peter.

ANNE What about it?

MRS FRANK Well, Daddy and I do trust you, you know, but ... *she hesitates*

ANNE Go on, then.

MRS FRANK Mrs van Daan ... she keeps saying things to me. It's not really fair to her to ... well, to keep Peter all to yourself.

ANNE *incredulously* You mean she's jealous!

MRS FRANK Well, you're so secretive, the two of you, up there in his room. And all the time, Anne; I just don't seem to be able to get through to you. Either that or you just make a joke of everything.

Anne *is silent.*

MRS FRANK Oh well, love can't be forced. I suppose. *She goes back to the table.*

SCENE FIFTEEN

As **Anne** *talks,* **Peter** *comes over and rearranges the rug, perhaps also bringing on a few cushions. A lighting effect of a barred window suggests* **Peter's** *attic room.*

ANNE My lighter, superficial side will always be too quick for the deeper side of me, and that's why it will always win. You can't imagine how often I've already tried to push this Anne away, to cripple her, to hide her, because after all, she's only half of what's called Anne. And Peter has touched my emotions more deeply than anyone else has ever done before – except in my dreams. Now even that's wrong, according to my parents!

Anne *moves towards* **Peter.**

ANNE Am I interrupting?

PETER No, of course not! I was just daydreaming. Taking a look at the history of the world through the window here.

ANNE That's a fine way of putting it – I must remember it. *She sits beside him.* All the arguments seem like sheer insanity when you're up here; it's so quiet.

PETER Do you know what I think? *He draws her head
down to rest against him.* That it is silly to fight with people
about whom you feel indifferent. To differ with people for
whom you care is another story. You are fond of them and it
hurts you more than it angers you when they provoke you.

ANNE But you don't quarrel much, do you?

PETER No, but enough to know what it's like.

Pause.

ANNE The worst of it is that most people go through this
world alone. I mean that, whether they're married or single,
they stand equally alone. They have no one with whom they
can talk about all of their feelings and thoughts.

---

*Music. As it plays, and as **Peter** and **Anne** sit, members of the
Chorus, dividing the lines between them, recite the following
poem, 'Colours', by Yevgeny Yevtushenko.*

CHORUS When your face
  appeared over my crumpled life
  at first I understood
  only the poverty of what I have.
  Then its particular light
  on woods, on rivers, on the sea,
  became my beginning in the coloured world
  in which I had not yet had my beginning.
  I am so frightened, I am so frightened,
  of the unexpected sunrise finishing,
  of revelations and tears and the excitement finishing.
  I don't fight it, my love is this fear,
  I nourish it who can nourish nothing,
  Fear hems me in.
  I am conscious that these minutes are short
  and that the colours in my eyes will vanish
  when your face sets.

ANNE *murmuring* It is the same for me.

PETER What's the matter? You're very serious. Laugh –
please laugh.

ANNE Why must I always laugh?

PETER Because I like it; you get such dimples in your cheeks when you laugh; how do they come, actually?

ANNE I was born with them. I've got one in my chin too – look! That's my only beauty.

PETER Of course not. That's not true.

ANNE Yes it is. I know quite well that I'm not a beauty; I never have been and never will be.

PETER I don't agree at all. I think you're pretty.

ANNE So are you then! *He laughs, pretending to hit her.*
Anne *comes forward.*

ANNE I hear a lot from all sides about the sudden friendship. Have our parents forgotten their own youth? It seems like it. *She returns to the rostrum and curls up in the blankets.*

SCENE SIXTEEN

Music: a quaint, 'wooden doll' Dutch folk melody, to represent Mrs van Daan, as Anne describes her.
    Mr and **Mrs van Daan** bring over a stool and chair to the central area. **Mr van Daan** sits on the chair reading a newspaper. **Mrs van Daan** sits facing front on the stool, as if at her mirror. She has taken off her apron and is putting on some ostentatious earrings.

MRS VAN DAAN Putti, where did you put my fur coat?

MR VAN DAAN Which fur coat?

MRS VAN DAAN That's a stupid question – I've only got one! . . . Putti . . . Why don't you answer?

MR VAN DAAN I thought you'd realise without my having to spell it out.

MRS VAN DAAN What do you mean?

MR VAN DAAN I've just said I didn't want to have to spell it out! Food! F–O–O–D! How do we get it? Coupons! C–O–U–P–O–N–S. What do we do when we run out?

MRS VAN DAAN You can't mean you've given it to Miep to sell!

MR VAN DAAN   Precisely!

MRS VAN DAAN   You're cruel, you really are cruel! How could you!

MR VAN DAAN   *warningly*   Kerli . . .

MRS VAN DAAN   What else is there to keep up our morale? Well . . .?

MR VAN DAAN   Every time Miep comes you want something to keep up your morale – soap, perfume. . . What about the rest of us?

MRS VAN DAAN   I've not asked for ages. I've got more sense!

MR VAN DAAN   I should hope so. People are starving out there now. We're the lucky ones!

MRS VAN DAAN   *incredulously*   The lucky ones?

MR VAN DAAN   You can't see anyone else's point of view but your own, can you? Miep tells us every day but you don't really listen! People are cutting down the trees or their doors for fuel, are eating cats because there's nothing else, cars are running on cooking gas if at all, bicycles have got wooden wheels, there's hardly any soap . . . People are so dirty they're covered in scabies. But you, always demanding something every inch of the way. They avoid coming upstairs to see *us*, Miep and Elli. They know what you're like!

MRS VAN DAAN   How can you say all these terrible things to me!

MR VAN DAAN   I'd soon know about it if the end was staring you in the face just because you preferred to starve than have your coat sold! *That'd* be pretty terrible wouldn't it!

MRS VAN DAAN   A terrible end is better than no end . . .

There is the sound of bombing, which continues during Scene Seventeen.

MRS VAN DAAN   *panics*   Putti . . .!

MR VAN DAAN   Now who's talking? Oh all right, we've heard it all before! We're still here.

SCENE SEVENTEEN

ANNE   *still from the rostrum*   Pim!

MR FRANK   All right, Anne! It's all right!

ANNE   Can you put the light on in my room?

32

MRS FRANK She's not a baby, Otto!

MR FRANK She's not exactly a veteran soldier either!

MRS VAN DAAN Mr Frank . . .!

MR FRANK Petronella van Daan . . . afraid of a few incendiaries?

MRS VAN DAAN There's a red glow in the window upstairs . . . the house has caught fire, I know it has!

MARGOT No, surely not, Mrs van Daan. We'd have heard the explosion here first.

MRS VAN DAAN I did.

ANNE It was right beside my bed.

MR FRANK It's very deceptive: you think it's happened right beside you when it's really streets away.

MRS FRANK Can you imagine the row if you were actually inside one of the planes!

MARGOT Miep says the milkman saw four Canadians sitting by the roadside yesterday. They'd parachuted out of their plane when it blew up. One of them asked him for a cigarette. Then the German police came and took them off.

MRS FRANK You don't know which are German planes and which are British ones. The bomb that finishes us off might be a British one. I sometimes wish it were all over quickly.

DUSSEL Nothing's going to finish us off, Mrs Frank. Come on now.

MARGOT Anne, what's that?

Anne *has moved over from the rostrum with a suitcase.*

ANNE It's my suitcase for getting out of here!

MRS FRANK *almost laughing* The street would be more dangerous! Where are you going to escape to?

ANNE I don't know, but there's nothing like hoping!

DUSSEL How about something to keep busy with rather than all standing here shivering.

MRS VAN DAAN *sarcastically* Go right ahead. We're all listening!

MR VAN DAAN Kerli . . .

DUSSEL Some exercises! *There is general protest at this.* But it's the best thing in the world for taking your mind off things!

ANNE Don't I know it! You should see him every Sunday morning. Just what I need to relax with!

DUSSEL   Oh come on, give it a try!

---

*Everyone starts to do exercises. **Anne** directs the others. General laughter. The sound of the bombs comes to an end.*

PETER   *referring to the bombs*   It's stopped.

MRS FRANK   We'll pay for this tomorrow, Mr Dussel. Just you wait till you're having to cook your own dinner because I'm laid up!

MARGOT   Don't you sometimes think that we'll be bored when the war ends and all this excitement is over?

MRS FRANK   I know what I'll do when it's all over – have some real coffee. What about you, Otto?

ANNE   I know what Pim will do – he'll want to rush off and see Elli's father in hospital. What do you want most of all when the war's over, Mrs van Daan?

MRS VAN DAAN   Cream cakes, immediately!

ANNE   Margot?

MARGOT   A hot bath!

MR VAN DAAN   Yes, I agree there. Overflowing, and I want to stay in it for at least half an hour.

MRS VAN DAAN   Peter's longing to get out to the pictures again. Did you notice the rash of beautiful movie stars on his wall?

PETER   Oh, Mother!

ANNE   I wouldn't know where to begin. I know one thing, though. I'd make sure I got something to wear before I went anywhere. This sweater's only mid-arm. And as for the buttons! Can you see me back at school in these, Pim?

MR FRANK   I'd see you back at school in almost anything, Anne.

*Everyone except **Anne** and **Mr Frank** moves back to sit at the table.*

ANNE   *hesitatingly*   Pim . . . can I talk to you? I'm worried about something.

MR FRANK   *gently*   Come on, then. Out with it.

ANNE   I expect you've guessed that when we're together, Peter and I don't sit miles apart . . . do you think it's wrong?

MR FRANK   No, I don't think it's wrong . . . but you must be careful, Anne. It is quite different from normal circumstances. You are bound to be so intense here. If you need to get away from each other – to see other young people – you can't.

ANNE   But I don't want to see anyone else!

MR FRANK   Well, there's the danger. It's so easy to get things all out of proportion, you know. I'm sure you both think you know you love each other now, but if one of you should change, where is the escape route?   *He moves over to the table.*

ANNE   *spotlit*   I am so frightened, I am so frightened
of the unexpected sunrise finishing,
of revelations and tears and the excitement finishing. . . .

I am conscious that these minutes are short
and that the colours in my eyes will vanish
when your face sets.

She joins the others.

SCENE EIGHTEEN

The family are once more seated round the table, dimly but warmly – almost cosily – lit.

   Miep *speaks from the back area. Soft, rather nostalgic music plays throughout* ***Miep's*** *speech.*

MIEP   All summer, round-ups of Jews continued in Amsterdam. Streets would be blocked off; soldiers would pull up the bridges and stand guard at intersections so no one could get away. All through the neighbourhood could be heard the shrill, piercing whistles, and then the sound of boots on steps, rifle butts on doors, insistent ringing of doorbells and the coarse, frightful voice demanding, Open up! Be quick! Be quick!
The annexe seemed a safe oasis from the dismal life in enemy-occupied Amsterdam. Each time I walked silently into the hiding-place I'd see each person engaged in activity. They looked like living cameos, a head lowered intently over a book,

hands poised over a pile of potato peelings, a dreamy look on a face whose hands were mindlessly knitting, a tender hand poised over Mouschi's silky back, stroking and touching, a pen scratching across a blank paper, pausing to chew over a thought, and then scratching again. All of them silent.

Lights up on annexe table.

ANNE *reading from diary* Dear Kitty, I suppose it's the van Daans' idea always to set me against my parents. Yesterday they told them that I was being allowed to read books that were far too old for me. I could have slapped their faces! Mrs van Daan is a nice one! She sets a fine example . . . she certainly sets one, a bad one. She is well-known for being very pushing, selfish, cunning, calculating and is never content. I could write whole chapters about Madame, and who knows, perhaps I will some day . . .

MRS VAN DAAN Hey Anne, can't I have a look?

ANNE I'm afraid not.

MRS VAN DAAN Just the last page then?

ANNE No, I'm sorry.

DUSSEL She's too modest to let you see it, Mrs van Daan.

MRS VAN DAAN Modest! Anne! She never lets herself be pushed around. Put it away, Anne; we'll have to make a start on the potatoes.

MRS FRANK You can't expect it of Anne if Peter doesn't, Mrs van Daan.

MRS VAN DAAN He's done enough to help me over the months. Besides, it's not appropriate work for boys.

MR FRANK If we all do it, I don't see why Peter shouldn't.

ANNE *aside to audience* The title of the next piece is 'The Battle of the Potatoes'.

*Short fanfare. During the next speech, the table is cleared and the others fetch the implements as **Anne** describes. **Margot** remains in the kitchen area, cleaning a pan.*

ANNE Why do grown-ups quarrel so easily and so much? Up till now I thought that only children squabbled, and that it wore off as you grew up! Here we go. One of us fetches the newspapers, another the knives, keeping the best for himself, of course, a third the potatoes, and the fourth a pan of water. Mr Dussel begins: he's the expert.

DUSSEL   Look, Anne, do it this way. I take the knife in my hand like this and scrape from the top downwards. No, not like that. Like this!

ANNE   I get on better like this, Mr Dussel.

DUSSEL   But still, this is the best way. You can take it from me!

MRS VAN DAAN   Putti, put on an apron. Tomorrow I shall have to get all the spots out of your suit.

MR VAN DAAN   I'm not getting myself dirty.

Pause

MRS VAN DAAN   Putti, why don't you sit down?

MR VAN DAAN   I'm comfortable standing up and I prefer it.

MRS VAN DAAN   You're making a mess! *sarcastically* Well, Margot, you must have had a lot to do!

MARGOT   There were all the pans, Mrs van Daan.

MRS FRANK   If there's just a little bit left you leave it in the pan, you know, Mrs van Daan. Then it goes bad and Margot has to scrape it off. It's not fair, you know. It does take a long time when the pan gets to that stage. Margot's entitled to her own time like the rest of us.

MRS VAN DAAN   Well, I don't see why the girls shouldn't spend more time helping with the real work instead of all this studying. There's no need for girls to learn so much. It gives them all sorts of vulgar ideas. It's not as if it made them any more docile or reserved. I'm sure Anne thinks she's being witty when really she's just plain rude. I'm the unassuming one around here. Like Mr Frank. You should take a leaf out of his book, Putti!

MRS FRANK   *dangerously* Surely you can't complain of their manners when they're sitting studying quietly and minding their own business, Mrs van Daan?

MR VAN DAAN   I don't wish to be modest. In my experience it doesn't pay. I know one thing: if I didn't look after myself I'd soon be starving!

MRS FRANK   I think I agree with you, Mr van Daan. Take my advice, Anne; don't be too unassuming – it doesn't get you anywhere.

MRS VAN DAAN   How can you sit there and say that to the girl! It was very different when I was young. And I feel sure that it still is, except in your modern home!

Anne *mimics her silently.*

MRS VAN DAAN   *furious*   Look at her! The insolence! If I could get my hands on her alone I'd give her such a slapping she wouldn't sit down for a week.

DUSSEL   Mrs van Daan – please! Quietly!

ANNE   Mr Dussel, the champion of youth!

MRS VAN DAAN   Don't you tell me what to say and what not to say!

DUSSEL   Remember where we are! It might be after 5.30 but there are limits to what sort of noise we can make!

MR FRANK   Mrs van Daan, in one respect Anne is extremely well brought up; she has learned one thing anyhow, and that's not to make any reply to your long sermons!

MRS FRANK   They don't deserve her attention. Look at the way you always tell Anne she ought to eat more vegetables and then take a minute helping yourself, because you say it'll make you constipated!

---

p. 58

Improvisation: the cat provides a diversion
Everyone's attention is diverted to a dripping coming from the ceiling, and to a strange smell. Peter's cat has 'misbehaved' upstairs and there are holes in the ceiling. **Peter** *begins to look distractedly round. He 'sees' the cat and chases it down the staircase. General hubbub and hilarity.*

MARGOT   It's all over everything, Pim: the potatoes and the books, and your birthday poem. The cat doesn't think much of anyone's work. There's poetic justice for you.

MR FRANK   Oh, do let's stop bickering and try to laugh a bit together.

ANNE   Margot, do read Pim's poem: it's very . . .   *searching for the word*   apposite.

MRS VAN DAAN   His poem?

ANNE   Yes. Pim always writes me a poem for my birthday, in German; then Margot translates it for me.

MARGOT   Though youngest here, you are no longer small,
But life is very hard, since one and all

38

Aspire to be your teacher, thus and thus:
'We know because we did it long ago.'
'Elders are always betters, you must know!'
At least that's been the rule since life began!
Our personal faults are much too small to scan;
This makes it easier to criticise
The faults of others, which seem double size!
Please bear with us, your parents, for we try
To judge you fairly and with sympathy.
Correction sometimes take against your will,
Though it's like swallowing a bitter pill,
Which must be done if we're to keep the peace.
While time goes by till all this suffering cease.
You read and study nearly all the day
Who might have lived in such a different way.
You're never bored, and bring us all fresh air.
Your only moan is this: 'What can I wear?
I have no knickers, all my clothes are small,
My vest might be a loin cloth, that is all!
To put on shoes would mean to cut off toes,
Oh dear, I'm worried by so many woes!'

SCENE NINETEEN

Peter stands at the top of the staircase.

PETER   Mr Frank, could you come here a minute!

Mr Frank and Mr van Daan join him and they go down the staircase.

ANNE   Now what's going on?

MRS FRANK   *at the top of the staircase – to Mr Frank*   What is it?

MR FRANK   *in a loud whisper, from the foot of the staircase*   Burglars – in the warehouse!

Noises from the back area.

MRS VAN DAAN   Surely we don't need to worry about that? I mean, it's terrible for the business but they're not going to come up here. They'll be after the stuff downstairs.

MARGOT   But the police will come if they see a break-in; they'll investigate everywhere!

MRS FRANK   Not every policeman would report us to the Nazis!

MARGOT   But if they see the radio – the dial's turned to the BBC and that's a criminal offence!

More noise

MRS VAN DAAN   What is it?

MR FRANK   *returning*   Just stay there. Turn the light down.

Mrs van Daan scrabbles frantically at the back of the stage. Lights dim suddenly. Mr Frank goes back downstairs.

ANNE   Not off, Mrs van Daan!

MRS FRANK   Oh no, where's the oil?

MRS VAN DAAN   I don't know – it was over here!

MRS FRANK   All right, never mind.

Silence

ANNE   Mother . . .

MRS FRANK   It's all right, Anne – I'm here.

ANNE   I keep hearing people – the Green Police coming for us.

MRS FRANK   That's just imagination.

ANNE   It isn't!

Peter comes back upstairs.

MARGOT   Quiet!

MRS FRANK   That's Peter coming back up.

ANNE   What happened?

PETER   There's a plank been bashed in – the top left-hand side of the outside door. We pushed it back and someone's just bashed it in again!

MR FRANK   *from the back area*   There's a torch!

In the back area there is a sudden beam of light illuminating Mr Frank and Mr van Daan. Here, D7 plays the part of the greengrocer. D10 is his wife.

MR VAN DAAN   Keep down!

D7 *from the back area* Come here, there's been a break-in.

D10 What's the building?

D7 Warehouse. Spice company – Travies and Co. They get their potatoes from me.

D10 You'd better call the police. With it being Easter Monday tomorrow no one will be here to repair it otherwise.

Mr van Daan and Mr Frank move up the staircase to join the others.

MR VAN DAAN They've sent for the police.

MR VAN DAAN I knew it!

MR FRANK The police could just as easily be good Dutch people as the NSB. Even if they are the NSB we can bribe them!

MARGOT We'll have to destroy the radio.

MRS VAN DAAN We'll have to burn Anne's diary as well. That tells them exactly who we are.

ANNE Not my diary. If that goes, I go as well.

Noise

MR FRANK There, they've gone. They never got further than the bookcase.

The lighting gradually returns to normal.

MRS VAN DAAN They could be back!

ANNE We must behave like soldiers, Mrs van Daan. If it's all up now, then let's go for Queen and country, for freedom, truth and right, as they say on Radio Orange. The only really awful thing is how many other people we'll get into trouble!

MARGOT I need the loo – the buckets are all in the attic. Pim, we can't go downstairs can we?

MR VAN DAAN There's Peter's waste-paper tin.

PETER Here you are, Margot.

MARGOT Is there any paper?

ANNE Here you are – I've got some in my pocket. It's got Marie Antoinette's family tree on. Hurry up, Margot; I need it too!

> *The others stand round **Margot** in the kitchen area, and then **Dussel** fetches the blankets from under the rostrum and distributes them.*
>
> *Lighting changes represent the passage of time throughout the next speech.*

ANNE   We all used the poor little tin, one after the other – that's what fear does to you! And then we tried to sleep. Mrs van Daan had her head on my foot, Dussel snored – I was used to that, of course! The tin soon began to smell ghastly. Mrs van Daan got up in the middle of the night and put chlorine in it, and a tea towel over the top.

The clock strikes eight o'clock.

In the morning, Daddy crept down to the office and phoned Miep.

SCENE TWENTY

> *__Miep__ comes up the staircase with a bag. **Anne** rushes over to her. The others stretch and yawn. The blankets are folded up.*

ANNE   Oh Miep!

MIEP   There, there, it's all over!

ANNE   I kept thinking the house was full of Gestapo!

MIEP   As it happens, it was just the night watchman and one policeman dragged in off his beat.

MR VAN DAAN   A couple came past and shone a torch in; I'm sure she said they were going to call the police.

MIEP   Just the greengrocer. I've just seen him as I came past. His wife wanted him to ring the police but he said he wanted to be on the safe side and that he didn't think it was the thing to do. He said he didn't know anything but guessed a lot. I'm sure he knows and is on our side. Henk's getting hold of Kraler and we'll get everything repaired as soon as possible.

MRS FRANK   What a night – we were sure it was the end. Come on now, cheer us up, Miep – you're the zoo-keeper!

MIEP   Well, I went to an engagement party.

PETER   What was there to eat?

MIEP   Oh, vegetable soup with minced meatballs – are you sure you want me to go on, Peter? Cheese, rolls, hors d'oeuvres, eggs and roast beef. . .

PETER   Eggs AND roast beef !!

MIEP   'Fraid so – and fancy cakes as well.

PETER   *groaning*   Do you know what we've been eating this weekend, apart from potatoes – kale, kale and more kale. It's supposed to have been preserved in its barrel, but it stinks! Two spoonfuls of porridge – that's breakfast. Rotten potatoes day after day, and lettuce, cooked or raw.

MRS VAN DAAN   And I have to cook without fats any more.

MIEP   I know, Mrs van Daan, I'm sorry. How they got that stuff I don't know. It must have been on the black market. Anyhow, something a bit more cheerful. It's not exactly an Easter bonnet, Anne, but you might appreciate it more.   *She hands Anne some shoes from the bag.*

ANNE   High heels!

MIEP   I just came across them and prayed they'd be the right size. . .

Anne tries them on and walks a few wobbly steps.

MRS FRANK   Oh, Anneliese! Miep, we haven't said anything about the optician yet – we wanted to give you more time to think about it.

ANNE   An optician. Have you found some glasses for me too, Miep? I bet I'll look a real owl!

MIEP   No, I can't just go in and get glasses for you. But the optician is only ten minutes away. I think I can get you out safely and back again. Your parents have agreed. We could get them ordered tomorrow if you like.

ANNE   Go outside the annexe?

SCENE TWENTY-ONE

*During the next speech **Anne** moves centre stage where she alone is lit. **Miep** leaves. **Margot** moves behind **Anne** to the rostrum where she replaces the blankets. The others are sitting by the table.*

ANNE   I want to be out there so much that whenever anyone comes in from the outside with the wind in their clothes and the cold on their faces I could bury my head in the blankets to stop myself longing. But I'd die with fear if you sent me out. Isn't it stupid! I'm such a coward.

*She moves over to sit beside **Margot** on the rostrum. The lights come up again.*

ANNE   Margot – do you ever wonder what we'll do with our lives when this is all over? What do you want to do?

MARGOT   Go to Palestine.

ANNE   What for?

MARGOT   Palestine's the place where we Jews could be ourselves. No one could put us into a category there. I'd like to be a midwife.

ANNE   How gory!

MARGOT   How about you, then?

ANNE   I want to go to Paris and study languages and art, or be a movie star.

MARGOT   Oh, Anne – I used to wish you'd be serious. Now I'm glad you're not.

ANNE   Margot, it's crazy. If I'm quiet and serious everyone thinks it's a new comedy so I have to turn it into a joke. Besides, I'm awfully scared that everyone who knows me as I always am will discover that really I have a nicer side, a finer side. I'm afraid that if they find it, they'll laugh at me and think I'm ridiculous and sentimental. Oh, I suppose I'm just feeling confused at the moment.

MARGOT   Peter?

ANNE   Yes.

MARGOT   Anyone can see he's beginning to be more and more in love with you.

ANNE   Oh, he longs to be loved all right.

MARGOT   And you're not so sure you love him. Is that what you mean?

ANNE   Well, things certainly aren't right between us at the moment. At least, not in my head they're not. I needed someone I could confide in.

MARGOT   You certainly seemed to be doing a lot of that!

ANNE   Margot, you're not jealous, are you? I would be if I were you. I mean, being the odd one out.

MARGOT   Oh Anne, I've never thought of Peter as anyone other than my younger brother. But you're right; I know I do feel the odd one out. A bit lonely, I suppose. I'd like someone to confide in as well.

ANNE   But the trouble is that I don't think I can share my thoughts with Peter to that extent. And I feel as if I've drawn him to me, not the other way round – that he's dependent on me. I can't see any way of shaking him off and . . . well, and putting him on his feet. I mean, suppose he asked me to marry him . . .

MARGOT   Oh Anne, you're only 15!

ANNE   Well, just suppose. When I was older.

MARGOT   Well, go on then. What would you do?

ANNE   I couldn't say yes, you know. He hasn't enough character yet, not enough will-power, too little courage and strength. He's only a child. But I'd find it hard to let him go.

MARGOT   There speaks Anne, the aged lady!

ANNE   Don't laugh at me, Margot. Am I really only 15? Am I really still a silly little schoolgirl? I've been through things that hardly anyone of my age has undergone.

*She moves forward. Spotlight on **Anne**.*

But even so my work, my hope, my courage . . . all these things keep my head above water and stop me complaining. Oh Kitty, there's such great commotion in the secret annexe at the moment. The Allies have invaded France and we're hoping that the war will be over by the end of the year! Now it doesn't concern the Jews any more; it concerns Holland and all occupied Europe. Perhaps I may yet be able to go back to school in September or October. In the meantime I must uphold my ideals, for perhaps the time will come when I shall be able to carry them out.

SCENE TWENTY-TWO

Banging of doors in the back area.

CONTROLLER 1 *from the back area* Open up!

CONTROLLER 2 Open up!

S1 Open up!

---

*The **Ss** sitting in front of the audience get up and move over to sweep the inhabitants of the annexe onto the rostrum. They stand around the rostrum facing outwards.*

CONTROLLER 2 *and **MIEP** stand facing each other, lit in the back area.*

CONTROLLER 2 Stay put, don't move. Aren't you ashamed to be helping Jewish garbage?

MIEP You're Viennese aren't you? I can tell. I'm from Vienna too.

CONTROLLER 2 Your papers. Identification.

MIEP Born in Vienna. Married to a Dutchman.

CONTROLLER 2 From personal sympathy, for you personally, you can stay. But God help you if you run away. Then we take your husband.

MIEP You will keep your hands off my husband. This is my business. He doesn't know anything about it.

CONTROLLER 2 Don't be so dumb – he must be involved in this too. I'll come back to make sure you're still here. One false move . . .

---

*Slow, sad music. Lights come up on the annexe area as **Miep** comes over to pile up the belongings. She finds the diary, faces out front, opens it . . . looks up and walks to the right of the stage.*

*The **Ds** walk up from the back area as the **Ss** move away to the sides of the rostrum. When in position around the entire stage area they remove their masks.*

46

SCENE TWENTY-THREE

Slides of the concentration camps accompany the next sequence. The music continues. Note: 'Chaim' is pronounced 'ch (as in 'loch') – eye-eem'.

MIEP   Almost every week a train left Westerbork holding camp for Auschwitz. Anne's family was on the very last one to go. If the family had been betrayed even just a week later things would have been very different.

D8   Lex van Weren, inmate of Auschwitz concentration camp . . .

S10   While we were on the train to Auschwitz the Green Police would grab anything they could get hold of . . . money, rings . . . anything. When they didn't get what they wanted they started hitting.

S4   In the freight trucks we were so crowded that we were each lying or sitting on top of each other. Even with this brutal treatment we still could not believe that at Auschwitz only death would await the majority.

D9   The weather was foggy and it was very early in the morning.

D10   The SS seemed to have waited to open the doors exactly until this hour, just between night and day. They hoped to confuse us, blind us with a futile hope.

S2   Polite music played.

The music changes.

S1   Before we realised it we were being marched along by the SS who ordered 'Left, right, right, left, left left,' left into the lorries, straight for the gas chambers.

S6   A bar was erected for the children. Those who could pass beneath it also went left, with the pregnant, women with babies, the elderly and the infirm.

D2   To the right went those of us capable of working on the land, capable of wielding a spade to dig the mass graves or of being experimented on to further the cause of science.

S5   We were stripped, shaved and had to give up all our meagre possessions.

D1   Devaluation.

The original sad music has re-established itself.

S3   Numbers were tattooed on our arms, striped prisoners' suits were flung at us in a heap and we were told to grab something quickly. If people weren't quick enough, there were the dogs.

S8   We were all given an identifying badge, of different colours and shapes, to show which category we fitted into.

S7   Chaim Natkiel, because of false identification papers, captured as a Christian working for the Dutch Resistance.

S5   The rest of my family were killed, 75 in all if you counted the brothers and sisters, grandparents, aunts and uncles, nieces and nephews and cousins.

---

*The **Chorus** moves to the back area, all except for six – **D7**, **D4**, **D3** included.*

D7   When I was liberated I joined hands with my five fellow Dutchmen and together we sang an old Dutch song – 'In Holland Stands a House'.

D4   Fed on two meals a day – 150 grams of bread for one, and a bowl of hot water with a vegetable leaf, called soup, for the other, Otto Frank ended up at the camp hospital at Auschwitz, where he still was when the camp was liberated by the Russians in 1945.

D3   Along with his fellows, he made his way back home . . .

The slide sequence ends.

*Six of the **Chorus** come forward – **D7**, **D4** and **D3** included. In a circle, they sing 'In Holland Stands a House'. (The words and music, are given at the back of the book. See page 82.) Simple actions accompany the song, perhaps ending with the singers forming an arch under which they lead off.*

*All the **Chorus** and the **Controllers** are now at the back. They quietly hang their masks up on the stand.*

***Miep** comes over to centre stage. During the next speech **Mrs Frank**, **Dussel** and the **van Daans** move off the rostrum and go through the audience to the back as their names are mentioned. Wistful music.*

MR FRANK   Miep, Edith's not coming back. She died in

Auschwitz. Dussel, the van Daans . . . van Daan I saw with my own eyes on his way to be gassed. Mrs van Daan, Peter, Dussel, I don't know. Margot and Anne were taken to Bergen-Belsen. Miep, it wasn't a death camp. In some deep part of me, like a rock, I count on their survival.

Anne and Margot have stepped off the rostrum. Anne moves upstage centre, back to audience, stage left of Miep.

MIEP Mr Frank had written for news to several Dutch people who, he learned, had been at Bergen-Belsen. Anne's 16th birthday was coming on June 12th . . . The birthday came and went. Then we got a letter from a nurse in Rotterdam . . .

Music ends.

D1 This is to testify that Margot and Anne Frank were in Block 19 at Bergen-Belsen camp, and died about the end of February, or the beginning of March, 1945. I myself was a prisoner in the same camp, in Block 1.

MIEP We understood later that both girls had caught typhus and died within a few days of each other. Shortly afterwards Bergen-Belsen was liberated. And I had something to give Otto Frank.

Margot moves to the back area. Anne turns and takes the diary Miep gives her. She hands it to Mr Frank.

Here is what Anne left you, Mr Frank . . .

ANNE *her voice is prerecorded* I wanted to go on living even after my death! And therefore I am grateful to God for giving me this gift, this possibility of developing myself and of writing, of expressing all that is in me.

Spotlight on Anne.

It really is a wonder I haven't dropped all my ideals because they seem so absurd and impossible to carry out. Yet I keep them, because in spite of everything I still believe that people are really good at heart.

MIEP Anne's story is a story of very ordinary people during extraordinary times. Times the like of which I hope with all my heart will never, never come again. It is for all of us ordinary people all over the world to see to it that they do not.

Music. As the spotlight fades on **Anne** *and* **Miep** *they withdraw, one to each side.*

The **Controllers** *carry forward the stand with the masks hanging on it and place it centre stage. The* **Controllers** *also withdraw.*

The music comes to an end with the masks spotlit.

STAGING THE PLAY

The style of the play is quite challenging. It mixes naturalistic scenes, such as the domestic scenes in the secret annexe, and a more documentary approach, in the sections which contain much important information. At times, the action becomes almost ritualistic, particularly in the final scene of the play. These elements are likely to be less obvious in a classroom reading of the text. The cast will need to make sure that their acting is appropriate for each particular section. There should be a clear contrast in voice, gesture and movement if the production is to achieve its full effect.

The play has an adaptable framework, which means you can add to it or alter it to suit your own interests and circumstances. The more you make the play your own, the more satisfying it will be.

A scene from the original production of the play

The Performance Space

You will need to look carefully at the performance space which is available before you decide on the best way to stage the play. In the original production the play was performed with the audience sitting in a semicircle round the acting area, with space behind them (designated 'the back area'). It could be performed more conventionally on a proscenium-arch stage, but, with increased distance from the action, the audience may lose the feeling of menace and tension which the production should try to create.

The Set

Above the rostrum, against the wall, is suspended a projection screen. In the original production there were sheets hanging to the right of this screen, painted with semi-abstract designs of barbed wire, prisoners, the Westerkirk clock outside the annexe, and so on. The exits were masked by movable display stands on which were mounted a display of photographs. Another idea for the display would be to include photographs of all the walls and barriers which have divided people, past and present, throughout the world. In the original production the display stands were in the centre of the acting area as the audience came in. Members of the cast moved the stands at the beginning of Act One.

Furniture should be kept to a minimum. You are not aiming for a realistic set. The coffee table, chairs and stools in the opening scenes must be reasonably elegant, whilst the furniture used during the scenes in the annexe should be more basic. Make a list of all the furniture you will need in the play, but be sure to keep your stage as flexible as possible.

Costume

The occupants of the annexe should be dressed to suit the period. Illustrated histories of the nineteen thirties and forties will be helpful here. After the interval, the cast can change into shabbier garments. In Scene Eight, the Frank family will need outdoor coats.

In the original production, the Chorus wore black 'leggings' and coloured tops; they had bare feet. Alternatively, they might wear jeans and coloured tee-shirts or sweaters; the 'S' or Swastika group might wear overalls, or look rather military.

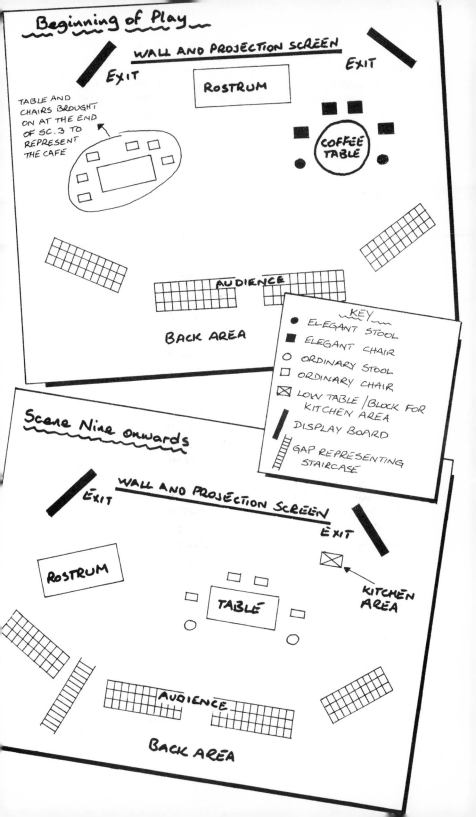

The 'D' or Star of David group could be dressed all in black. The most vital feature of their costumes are the masks they wear throughout. The 'D' group could have yellow masks, and those wearing Swastikas, black. The Controllers could have the colour of their choice: red works well.

Masks

The masks can be as simple or sophisticated as you want to make them. You could cut them out of cardboard, or perhaps mould them in papier mâché. For the original production, a technique using strips of plaster of paris bandage was used. In this method, the mask is made on the face of the actor: tie the hair back and cover the forehead, nose and cheeks with a layer of cold cream. Build up the structure of the mask with thin strips of plaster of paris bandage soaked in water. Take the mask down to the level of the nose and out from each side. After about 20 to 30 minutes it should be possible to ease the mask off the face. When the mask is dry, seal it with some strong rubber-based adhesive. When it has dried again it can be painted. Staple strips of material to the sides for ties to hold the mask in position.

Properties

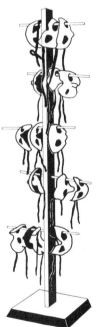

Make a careful list of all the props that are used in the play, for example books, newspapers, kitchen equipment, etc. Decide which props are essential, and which you will add to 'dress' the set, bearing in mind that all the belongings used in the annexe will need to be carried in the suitcases.

An essential prop is the stand on which the masks worn by the Chorus are hung at the end of the play, as on a war memorial. This can be made very simply from two pieces of wood and a few lengths of dowel, as shown in the illustration. You may, of course, prefer to build a stand to your own design.

In Scene Eleven a home-made menorah (eight-branched candlestick) is required. Jewish children frequently make these at school; it would be an interesting exercise to find out the method used today. Alternatively, you could copy the basic design in the illustration.

Stand for masks

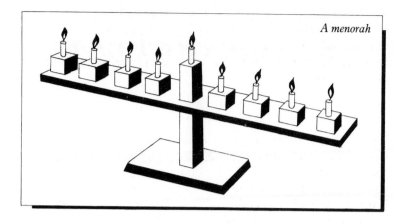

A menorah

Music

Music was an integral part of the original production – as a background to some of the dialogue and to represent the passage of time. Music will help to create the right atmosphere, so be careful what you choose to play even before the play begins. You might enjoy choosing extracts from existing works – or composing your own music for your production. There are opportunities for including your own songs, for example at the end of Scene Seven. Some of the music used in the original production is included at the end of the book.

Slide projection

Material for slide projection (in particular, views of the interior of the annexe) can be obtained from the Anne Frank Foundation, Prinsengracht 263, 1016GV Amsterdam. It would be a useful project for the production team to research other pictures to be photographed and projected. Drawings are another possibility, and would photograph more easily. It would be possible to perform the play without slide projection if this is too difficult. A sense of atmosphere can be created by lighting the different acting areas carefully.

IMPROVISATIONS WITHIN THE PLAY

There are several moments in the play which are not scripted in detail and which require the actors to improvise some of the actions and dialogue.

Some improvisations will need more careful preparation than others, but they are presented here in the order in which they appear in the play.

The family photograph   Scene One

Organisation: Work in groups of five or three. One of you is the photographer, the other four are Mr and Mrs Frank, Anne and Margot, or just Anne and Margot if there are only three in the group.

Situation: The photographer is trying to put his subjects at ease. He chats to them about their jobs, their interests, their names and, in the case of Anne and Margot, their ages.

As the family members take up their positions, what can we learn about their relationship to each other? Make sure that if the family pose for a series of photos, each new position reveals something more about each one of them.

Packing   Scene Eight

Organisation: Work with a partner. Imagine that one of you is Anne and the other is Margot.

Situation: Anne and Margot are packing their most vital belongings into a school satchel to take with them into the annexe. Anne puts in her diary, hair curlers, some handkerchiefs, schoolbooks, a comb and some old letters – things that are important to her. Margot is aware that the family may be in hiding for some time. She knows that it will only be possible to take with them what they can carry. She encourages Anne to pack sensible things, while at the same time trying to decide what to take for herself.

When they have almost finished packing, Anne mentions her cat, Moortie. Margot tries to explain why it will be impossible to bring the cat.

Improvise this scene, and try to let your conversation reveal the different characters of the two girls. Anne is impulsive and rather immature, while Margot is more grown-up, with a greater realisation of what lies ahead.

Saying goodbye   Scene Eight ⟨p. 17⟩

Organisation: Work with a partner. Imagine that one of you is Margot, and the other is Anne.

Situation: The family are about to leave their home. Imagine that Anne is holding her cat Moortie, who is to be left behind with neighbours, and saying goodbye to her. Margot is watching her sympathetically.

Anne's farewell to her cat should be quite touching. If you include this scene in the play, it will be important that the audience are convinced of the imaginary cat's existence. It can be difficult to improvise by yourself. Ask your partner, who is watching as 'Margot', to give you feedback on the effectiveness of your monologue.

Daily life   Scene Eleven ⟨p. 22⟩

Organisation: Work in groups of seven – all the occupants of the annexe except Anne.

Situation: It is a typical evening in the annexe. Everyone is busy with their own activities. Each person should decide what their character would be likely to be doing – reading, cooking, knitting.

There are several ways of presenting this scene. It could be improvised briefly using dialogue, or be presented without any words. Another idea is to show a series of tableaux or 'frozen pictures' of the life of the annexe.

The giving of presents   Scene Eleven ⟨p. 24⟩

Organisation: Work in a group of eight, as the occupants of the annexe. Decide what present each of them might have received.

Situation: The box of presents brought by Miep is distributed. Everyone receives an appropriate gift and thanks Miep. (Peter receives a cap.)

The presents should be simple and homemade. It might be possible for other presents, and other family gatherings, to be remembered as the gifts are shared. Do you think this would be a happy or a sad occasion?

The cat provides a diversion **Scene Eighteen**

Organisation: Work in groups of eight – the inhabitants of the annexe.

Situation: Peter's cat has misbehaved upstairs. Everyone reacts to this in a different way.

This incident occurs during a quarrel. It will be important that the interruption is enough to take everyone's mind off what they've been arguing about. The scene needs to be improvised with a great deal of energy, so that a real 'diversion' is created.

Activities On And Around The Play

Decisions

Organisation: Work in a small group. Imagine that, like Mr and Mrs Frank, you are all people with responsibilities for young families, who have to decide what to do in the face of approaching danger.

Situation: One of you believes that there is very little time left, and that the safest thing to do is to go into hiding. Can you persuade the rest of the group to hide also?

First line: **'We haven't much time ...'**

What about the risks?

Organisation: Work with a partner. One of you is Miep, or perhaps one of the other people who helped the Franks. You have decided that you must do everything you can to help them in hiding. Your partner is a close relative, maybe a husband or wife.

Situation: Tell your relative what you plan to do. You may have to persuade them that it is the right thing to do, and that you are well aware of the risks involved. Will your partner try to change your mind, or will you get a great deal of support?

First line: **'I've got something to tell you ...'**

Where's Anne?

Organisation: Work in a group of two or three. Imagine that you are all friends of Anne and Margot.

Situation: One of you has seen the Frank family making their way through the streets with their belongings. Another friend suspects that they may have gone into hiding, but knows that it may be dangerous to discuss this. Someone in the group might have been indiscreet or belong to a family with pro-Nazi sympathies.

First line: **'Have you seen Anne or Margot?'**

In hiding

Organisation: Work with a partner. Imagine that you are both young people in a similar situation to that of Anne and Margot.

Situation: You have been told that you may have to go into hiding. Think of a place in your home or neighbourhood – an attic or cellar, or perhaps an outhouse – where you might hide. Discuss your ideas with a partner, and decide on the best hiding-place.

Planning: Work out whether your chosen hiding-place will have electricity, a toilet and running water. Make a list of the basic things you would need to provide for your hiding-place. Essential items might include:
- bedding
- a stove or cooker
- a sink or some means of washing

Categories: Divide these items into categories: necessities and those things you will need for relaxation. Try to put everything down. Once you are in hiding, it will be impossible to return for things you may have forgotten.

The attic of the annexe

I forgot …

Organisation: Work with a small group – perhaps another pair. Share your list of items. Have you forgotten anything vital to your comfort and survival?

Situation: The four of you are in hiding together. Prepare a scene which shows what might happen when the group discovers that some essential item has been left behind.

First line: **'Where did you put the …?'**

Only ten things ...

Organisation: Work with a partner. Look at your list of items. Now, each of you should go through your list of things separately until you have selected ten items which you feel you can't leave behind. These must be things which you can carry with you, perhaps in a small satchel or bag. Check your list with your partner's list.

Situation: Try to explain and justify to your partner why you have chosen certain things.

First line: **'I can't possibly leave this behind ...'**

A process of elimination

Organisation: Stay with the same partner.

Situation: Imagine that you are now only allowed ten items *between you*, although you will be allowed one extra luxury item each. How will you decide what to leave behind?

Essentials

Discussion: Compare your list with those made by other people in the class. What can you discover about the kinds of things which are important to most people?

Where did you put my fur coat?

Organisation: In the play, Mrs van Daan's fur coat is sold to buy food. Work in a small group. Look again at the items which are on your list. Is there anything which could be sold or exchanged for food, medicine or fuel – things which might be necessary to the survival of someone in the group?

Situation: Prepare and show a short scene in which one person in the group has to part with something very precious to them. Make sure that the circumstances show how this step is inevitable.

First line: **'We have to make a decision ...'**

Venturing outside

Organisation: Work in a small group. Imagine that Anne does actually leave the annexe to get spectacles, a possibility that Miep mentions in Scene Twenty. One of the group will be Anne, another will be the optician, a third could be Miep, and a fourth might be a sociable customer.

Situation: Improvise the scene in the optician's. What will the optician say to make polite conversation with Anne? Will the war be a topic for discussion, or rumours about the fate of the Jews? Will Anne's identity be suspected? What will Anne say if she is questioned about her life? Will Miep be able to help her?

First line: **'Do you live nearby?'**

Dreams of the future

Organisation: Look again at Scene Seventeen, where the occupants of the annexe discuss what they intend to do as soon as the war is over. Work in a group of four or five.

Situation: Create a tableau (a frozen picture) of an idyllic scene which might be the kind of moment that the occupants of the annexe would dream about. Decide whether your tableau will focus on food, on freedom or relationships.

Sharing: Share your tableau with other groups. Give each tableau a title.

There's no need for girls to learn so much ...

Writing: Anne had to try hard not to retaliate when Mrs van Daan criticised her parents for bringing up a girl to work hard at her studies rather than to concentrate on the household tasks. Imagine she had vented her feelings on the subject in a letter to Mrs van Daan, not intended to be sent but to be included in her diary as an expression of how she felt. Read the scenes in the play where domestic quarrels arise (Scenes Thirteen and Eighteen).

Are there still inequalities today in the way in which boys and girls are brought up? If you feel that things might be arranged more fairly in your own home, write a letter to your parents in which you suggest some changes.

Deprivation

Research: In Scene Sixteen, Mr van Daan describes the hardships endured by the ordinary people in Holland. Do you know anyone who lived through World War Two? Make enquiries among elderly members of your family or friends who may have had to endure similar hardships or deprivation.

Passing the time

Discussion: Margot, Peter and Anne try to use the lonely time they spend in the annexe profitably. Anne describes how she sets herself to study and to read as much as possible. Soldiers who were prisoners of war often used the time to study, keep fit and learn new skills. If you were in a similar situation, maybe through illness rather than political disaster, what programme of study would you draw up for yourself? Perhaps you could learn a new craft or skill, or improve in an area you know about already. You would have to allow yourself some basic books, instruments or tools.

Where do you draw the line?

Discussion: In the Preface to the play it says that even Anne herself can be guilty of intolerance. Find examples in the play of Anne's lack of understanding of other people.

Which of your own bad habits do you think would cause most irritation to people around you if you were in Anne's situation? Which qualities in other people generally do you find irritating?

What issues in society make you feel really outraged, as opposed to just irritated? Consider the smaller issues as well as the larger ones.

Do you think that there are some things about which we ought to feel outraged? Or should we too be tolerant about everything? What happens when people's personal liberties come into conflict? For example, is one person's freedom to smoke more important than another person's freedom to have clean air? Where do you draw the line? If you don't draw it somewhere you may find yourself saying that Adolf Hitler was perfectly entitled to his own prejudices; there are some people who do subscribe to this point of view.

The real you

Writing: Anne spoke in her diary about being a 'dual personality':

"...My lighter, superficial side will always be too quick for the deeper side of me and that's why it will always win. You can't imagine how often I've already tried to push this Anne away, to cripple her, to hide her, because after all, she's only half of what's called Anne."

Think about your own personality in the light of this. You may often have been asked to write about yourself. This time, try writing about yourself as different people might see you – a parent, a brother or sister, a friend, a teacher, the local shopkeeper, etc.

Peter van Daan

Anne and Peter

Discussion: Anne's feelings for Peter underwent many changes during the stay in the annexe. She almost despised him when they first went into hiding. Later, she came to love him. Finally, she was disappointed in him.

Re-read the poem in Scene Fifteen. It is called 'Colours', by Yevgeny Yevtushenko and is translated from the Russian.

Do you think the poet has been successful in expressing the feelings of people who have just fallen in love? What are their fears? Why might Anne share them?

Look back at Scene Seventeen. Do you think Mr Frank is correct in what he says to Anne? At least, do you think he was wise to say what he did?

REFUGEE BLUES

Discussion and Writing

1   Read the poem on pages 66 and 67 carefully. 'Refugee Blues' is not the original title of the poem. Do you think it is a good title?

2   The poet refers not only to those killed in the Holocaust (the name given to the deliberate extermination of so many people by the Nazis), but also to all those displaced people left after the war without home or country.

● What groups of people are in a similar position in the world today?
● Discuss the reasons for their situation – for example war, famine, racial hatred.
● What is being done by other countries to help them?
● Find out as much as you can about the plight of today's refugees.
● Set up a class debate about the question of the responsibility of developed nations towards those countries or groups of people who need medical, financial or military assistance, or economic, religious or political asylum. If you like, you can choose a real case from current events to discuss.

3   Look again at the second verse. Are there any countries in the world which have lost their sovereignty as separate states, have been renamed or have had their traditions and cultures suppressed?

4   Write in your own words about some of the situations in the poem which seem to you to be particularly unfair. You will find that you have to use far more words than the poet did. In poetry it is possible to express ideas very concisely.

5   Choose one of the situations described in the poem and write about it in another style – for example, a newspaper account, an official report, or a paragraph from a novel about refugees.

6   'Blues' usually refers to a song. This poem was set to music for the first production of the play. Think of a tune you know which might fit these words, or compose a tune of your own to fit the poem.

7   Try to find a modern song which deals with similar themes or expresses the same kinds of feelings as this poem.

Verse Speaking

Work in a small group. Experiment with different ways of saying this poem aloud. Decide how you will allocate the lines. Should a different person speak each verse? How will you handle the repetitions? You could consider speaking the poem, instead of singing it, in a production of the play.

Dance Drama

1   Would it add to the effect of the poem if some of you could act it out in mime while others spoke the verse?

2   Make a list of the different images which come to your mind when you read the poem. Work in a small group and create a series of tableaux (frozen pictures) to accompany the poem. Again, you might find ways of using these tableaux in a production of the play.

3   When you are really familiar with the poem, work together to create a dance drama based on the ideas and images in the poem. Decide how you will get a balance and a contrast between groups and individuals, what images you will try to convey exactly, and which can be represented non-verbally. Select music to accompany your dance drama, and share your work with others in the class.

1*   Say this city has ten million souls,
  Some are living in mansions, some are living in holes:
  Yet there's no place for us, my dear, yet there's no place for us.

2*   Once we had a country and we thought it fair,
  Look in the atlas and you'll find it there:
  We cannot go there now, my dear, we cannot go there now.

3*   In the village churchyard there grows an old yew,
  Every spring it blossoms anew:
  Old passports can't do that, my dear, old passports can't do that.

4*   The consul banged the table and said:
  'If you've got no passport you're officially dead':
  But we are still alive, my dear, but we are still alive.

5*   Went to a committee; they offered me a chair;
  Asked me politely to return next year:
  But where shall we go today, my dear, but where shall we go today?

6*   Came to a public meeting; the speaker got up and said:
'If we let them in, they will steal our daily bread';
He was talking of you and me, my dear, he was talking of you
    and me.

7   Thought I heard the thunder rumbling in the sky;
It was Hitler over Europe, saying: 'They must die';
O we were in his mind, my dear, O we were in his mind.

8*   Saw a poodle in a jacket fastened with a pin,
Saw a door opened and a cat let in:
But they weren't German Jews, my dear, but they weren't
    German Jews.

9*   Went down to the harbour and stood upon the quay,
Saw the fish swimming as if they were free:
Only ten feet away, my dear, only ten feet away.

10   Walked through a wood, saw the birds in the trees;
They had no politicians and sang at their ease:
They weren't the human race, my dear, they weren't the
    human race.

11   Dreamed I saw a building with a thousand floors,
A thousand windows and a thousand doors;
Not one of them was ours, my dears, not one of them was
    ours.

12*   Stood on a great plain in the falling snow;
Ten thousand soldiers marched to and fro:
Looking for you and me, my dear, looking for you and me.

W. H. Auden

The verses marked with an asterisk were used in the original
production of the play. You will find the music they were set to on
pages 80 and 81.

A refugee family

67

DIARY ENTRIES

1   Imagine that Anne had time to write one more entry in her diary between the time that the Germans arrived and the time that the family were marched out of the annexe. Compose this entry yourself.

2   Imagine that any of the other characters in the annexe also kept a diary. There are endless possibilities here.

- Mrs van Daan's outpourings might be the easiest to start with, and it would be interesting to explore the idea that Anne was perhaps very unfair in her judgement of this woman, who is described by Miep as a very good cook and generous enough to give her a beautiful ring as a thank-you present on her birthday, even though it would have bought the van Daans much-needed food and clothes on the black market. Try to think how Mrs van Daan might have written about the events in Scene Sixteen, or Scenes Eighteen and Nineteen.

- Mr Dussel would also have much to say about Anne in his diary. Don't forget that Miep describes him as 'a handsome man, a charmer, a very appealing person . . . cultivated and highly intelligent'. Her husband, Henk, recalled the story of two airmen who were once stranded in Antarctica after making an emergency landing; one of them is reported to have said that it was not the loneliness that had nearly driven him mad but the noise that the other man had made each day as he cleared his throat, and the way he had folded up his trousers! Maybe Anne and Mr Dussel got on each other's nerves in similar ways.

- Margot and Mrs Frank might also have said some revealing things about their relationship with Anne if they had kept diaries. How might Mrs Frank have recalled Anne's snub in Scene Fourteen, and how might Margot have felt about their conversation in Scene Twenty-one? Did either of them understand Anne well? Try to consider these points as you write your diary entries for these characters.

3 If you have never kept a diary yourself, try keeping one for a week. It may help to imagine, like Anne, that you are writing to a friend. Give the friend a name.

4 Anne Frank's *Diary* has sold millions of copies throughout the world. Can you think of any other famous diaries, fact or fiction, which have been bestsellers? You probably know *The Secret Diary of Adrian Mole*. It may seem to have very little in common with Anne Frank's diary; *Adrian Mole* was written as fiction and is, of course, very funny. Why do you think the two books have been so popular? Can you see *any* similarities between them? Can you explain how diaries can catch people's imagination and why they become so very popular?

Anne Frank in 1940

ANNE FRANK HUIS

Even now, after twice her lifetime of grief
and anger in the very place, whoever comes
to climb these narrow stairs, discovers how
the bookcase slides aside, then walks through
shadow into sunlit rooms, can never help

but break her secrecy again. Just listening
is a kind of guilt: the Westerkirk repeats
itself outside, as if all time worked round
towards her fear, and made each stroke
die down on guarded streets. Imagine it –

three years of whispering and loneliness
and plotting, day by day, the Allied line
in Europe with a yellow chalk. What hope
she had for ordinary love and interest
survives her here, displayed above the bed

as pictures of her family; some actors;
fashions chosen by Princess Elizabeth.
And those who stoop to see them find
not only patience missing its reward,
but one enduring wish for chances

like my own: to leave as simply
as I do, and walk at ease
up dusty tree-lined avenues, or watch
a silent barge come clear of bridges
settling their reflections in the blue canal.

Andrew Motion

Read the poem carefully. Why do you think Scene Nine of the play begins with a guided tour of the annexe? There were some practical reasons, but this poem may help to suggest some ideas that are less obvious.

Discuss or write about the following questions:

1   When do you think the poem was written? (Look at lines 1 and 2.)

2   What do you think the author means in referring to listening as 'a kind of guilt'?

3   '. . . . not only patience missing its reward
    but one enduring wish for chances
    like my own. . . . .'
    What differences between Anne's situation and his own does the poet record in the last verse?

The front of the building where Anne was in hiding

71

GOOD FENCES MAKE GOOD NEIGHBOURS

In the Prologue to the play the Controllers teach the Chorus to repeat the line, 'Good fences make good neighbours'. Read the poem from which the line is taken.

Mending Wall

Something there is that doesn't love a wall,
That sends the frozen-ground-swell under it,
And spills the upper boulders in the sun;
And makes gaps even two can pass abreast.
The work of hunters is another thing:
I have come after them and made repair
Where they have left not one stone on a stone,
But they would have the rabbit out of hiding,
To please the yelping dogs. The gaps I mean,
No one has seen them made or heard them made,
But at spring mending-time we find them there.
I let my neighbour know beyond the hill;
And on a day we meet to walk the line
And set the wall between us once again.
We keep the wall between us as we go.
To each the boulders that have fallen to each.
And some are loaves and some so nearly balls
We have to use a spell to make them balance:
"Stay where you are until our backs are turned!"
We wear our fingers rough with handling them.
Oh, just another kind of outdoor game,
One on a side. It comes to little more:
There where it is we do not need the wall:
He is all pine and I am apple orchard.
My apple trees will never get across
And eat the cones under his pines, I tell him.
He only says, "Good fences make good neighbours."
Spring is the mischief in me, and I wonder
If I could put a notion in his head:
"Why do they make good neighbours? Isn't it

Where there are cows? But here there are no cows.
Before I built a wall I'd ask to know
What I was walling in or walling out,
And to whom I was like to give offence.
Something there is that doesn't love a wall,
That wants it down." I could say "Elves" to him,
But it's not elves exactly, and I'd rather
He said it for himself. I see him there
Bringing a stone grasped firmly by the top
In each hand, like an old-stone savage armed.
He moves in darkness as it seems to me,
Not of woods only and the shade of trees.
He will not go behind his father's saying,
And he likes having thought of it so well
He says again, "Good fences make good neighbours."

Robert Frost

Discussion

1 Re-read lines 1–3. How do you know that even nature resists the idea of having barriers erected between people?

2 What does Robert Frost say to his neighbour to try to convince him that there is no need for a wall?

3 Why do you think his neighbour felt a wall was necessary, even so?

4 Which phrase near the end of the poem shows us that Frost thinks his neighbour's attitude was rather barbaric and uncivilised?

5 What do you think Frost means when he says of his neighbour: 'He will not go behind his father's saying'?

6 In what ways can you compare the attitude of Frost's neighbour to the attitude of other people who are prejudiced?

7 Re-read Scenes One, Three, Four, Five and Seven in the play, where the Nazis' attacks on the Jews are described. Do you think that Hitler's actions were the logical extension of the idea of building fences and walls between people?

8 Why do you think the characters in the Chorus are handed armbands and swastikas when they enter? Why would the same point not have been made so clearly if they had come on stage wearing them?

9 In the Prologue, the Controller is rather like the father of Frost's neighbour, who taught his son an idea which was really rather senseless but which, in time, Frost's neighbour came to accept as true. What do you think would have happened if one of the Chorus had refused to cooperate with the Controller?

10 How does Scene One follow on from this opening sequence?

Research
If you were designing the scenery for the play, or the display boards suggested in the description of the set on page 52, what walls or barriers known throughout the world to divide people might you show? You will probably need to do some research here.

Writing
Have you ever had arguments with neighbours, either at home or at school, over a line of demarcation in some form or another? This may have involved articles or objects which one of you thinks it is quite acceptable to share and the other does not. Write an account of your experiences in play or story form, or imagine a situation which could occur in your neighbourhood and write a newspaper account of it.

FEAR

This story by Anne Frank is published in the book *Anne Frank's Tales from the Secret Annexe*. Read it carefully, and then re-read Scene Seventeen of the play.

How much of Anne's own situation is reflected in her writing here? What do we learn about the real Anne from this fictional account of a girl's fear and flight? The character in her story found peace in the quiet of the countryside. How might Anne's love of nature have helped her while she was shut up from the world for more than two years?

25 March 1944

It was a terrible time through which I was living. The war raged about us, and nobody knew whether or not he would be alive the next hour. My parents, brothers, sisters, and I made our home in the city, but we expected that we either would be evacuated or have to escape in some other way. By day the sound of cannon and rifle shots was almost continuous, and the nights were mysteriously filled with sparks and sudden explosions that seemed to come from some unknown depth.

I cannot describe it; I don't remember that tumult quite clearly, but I do know that all day long I was in the grip of fear. My parents tried everything to calm me, but it didn't help. I felt nothing, nothing but fear; I could neither eat nor sleep – fear clawed at my mind and body and shook me. That lasted for about a week; then came an evening and a night which I recall as though it had been yesterday.

At half past eight, when the shooting had somewhat died down, I lay in a sort of half doze on a sofa. Suddenly all of us were startled by two violent explosions. As though stuck with knives, we all jumped up and ran into the hall. Even Mother, usually so calm, looked pale. The explosions repeated themselves at pretty regular intervals. Then: a tremendous crash, the noise of much breaking glass, and an earsplitting chorus of yelling and screaming. I put on what heavy clothes I could find in a hurry, threw some things into a rucksack, and ran. I ran as

75

fast as I could, ran on and on to get away from the fiercly burning mass about me. Everywhere shouting people darted to and fro; the street was alight with a fearsome red glow.

I didn't think of my parents or of my brothers and sisters. I had thoughts only for myself and knew that I must rush, rush, rush! I didn't feel any fatigue; my fear was too strong. I didn't know that I had lost my rucksack. All I felt and knew was that I had to run.

I couldn't possibly say how long I ran on with the image of the burning houses, the desperate people and their distorted faces before me. Then I sensed that it had got more quiet. I looked around and, as if waking up from a nightmare, I saw that there was nothing or no one behind me. No fire, no bombs, no people. I looked a little more closely and found that I stood in a meadow. Above me the stars glistened and the moon shone; it was brilliant weather, crisp but not cold.

I didn't hear a sound. Exhausted, I sat down on the grass, then spread the blanket I had been carrying on my arm, and stretched out on it.

I looked up into the sky and realized that I was no longer afraid; on the contrary, I felt very peaceful inside. The funny thing was that I didn't think of my family, nor yearn for them; I yearned only for rest, and it wasn't long before I fell asleep there in the grass, under the sky.

When I woke up the sun was just rising. I immediately knew where I was; in the daylight I recognized the houses at the outskirts of our city. I rubbed my eyes and had a good look around. There was no one to be seen; the dandelions and the clover-leaves in the grass were my only company. Lying back on the blanket for a while, I mused about what to do next. But my thoughts wandered off from the subject and returned to the wonderful feeling of the night before, when I sat in the grass and was no longer afraid.

Later I found my parents, and together we moved to another town. Now that the war is over, I know why my fear disappeared under the wide, wide heavens. When I was alone with nature, I realized – realized without actually knowing it – that fear is a sickness for which there is only one remedy. Anyone who is as afraid, as I was then, should look at nature and see that God is much closer than most people think.

Since that time I have never been afraid again, no matter how many bombs fell near me.

NEVER AGAIN?

Discussion

Look again at the last stage direction in the play. Why do you
think the author intended the masks to be removed and
displayed in this way at the end of the play? It may help to
consider what happens during the ceremony at the Cenotaph
(the memorial to the dead of two World Wars) in London, on
Remembrance Sunday.

Do you think there is anything to be gained by observing such
customs as these? After all, we are tempted to think that such
terrible events could never happen again.

Now read this poem, which is by Geoffrey Summerfield.

1945

The news was of inhumanity,
Of crimes, obscenities,
Unspeakable insanity
And bestial atrocities.

Somebody turned the radio down.
Nobody said a word.
Auschwitz, Buchenwald, and Belsen:
'It couldn't happen here,' they said.

At school the teacher set revision:
Of the princes murdered in the tower,
The Spanish Inquisition,
And Genghis Khan drunk with power;

Of heretics, burnt at the stake,
Refusing to deny a vow;
Mass-murders for religion's sake;
He said, 'It couldn't happen now.'

'You're next,' the school-bullies snigger,
'Don't try any silly tricks!'
All through History he tries to figure
A way out of punches and kicks.

At the end of morning-school,
They drag him to an air-raid shelter.
Down into darkness, damp and cool,
With Puncher and Kicker and Belter.

They tear off all his clothes
And tread them on the floor.
With obscenities and oaths,
They let him have what-for.

Their tortures are very crude,
Clumsy and unrefined.
With a sudden change of mood
They pretend to be friendly and kind.

They change their tack once more
And punch him black and blue.
He ends, crouched on the floor,
And finally they're through.

With a special parting kick
They warn him not to talk.
He feels wretched, sore and sick,
Gets up, can hardly walk.

*A National Front march
in England in 1984*

It's a beautiful Summer day,
His eyes squint in the sun.
He hears two passing women say,
'Oh, schooldays are such fun.'

Words echo in his head:
'Couldn't happen here,' they said.
And 'Couldn't happen now,' they said.
He never breathes a word.

Geoffrey Summerfield

What happened?

Organisation: Work with a partner. Imagine that one of you is the boy in the poem, and the other is a teacher.

Situation: The teacher has noticed that the child has bruises. Is it possible to get the child to talk about what happened?

First line: **'I know there's something wrong ...'**

Responsibility

Organisation: Work in a group of five or six. You are all members of staff in the school.

Situation: The level of bullying in the school is rising dangerously. Is there anything the teachers can do about it? Whose responsibility is it to prevent this kind of activity?

First line: **'It's just high spirits ...'**

Discussion

Can you find examples of this continuing intolerance, inhumanity and indifference to human suffering in recent TV news reports or in the newspapers? Is there anything that ordinary people can do about these terrible events?

It may seem that to remember the misery endured by the victims of 'man's inhumanity to man' is to dwell on horror unnecessarily. Miep did not think so:

'My story is a story of very ordinary people during extraordinary times. Times the like of which I hope with all my heart will never, never come again. It is for all of us ordinary people all over the world to see to it that they do not.'

MUSIC

Refugee Blues
Verses 1 and 12 are sung to accompaniment A.
In verse 4, the first two lines are spoken over accompaniment A.
The last line is sung.
Verses 2, 3, 5, 8 and 9 are sung to accompaniment B.
Verse 6 also uses accompaniment B, but the second line should
be spoken.

ACCOMPANIMENT B

© *Lucy Rogers 1989*

81

In Holland Staat Een Huis
(IN HOLLAND STANDS A HOUSE)

Adapted from an old Dutch song.

Translation

1: In Holland stands a house . . . (repeat and chorus)
2: In the house there lives a child . . . (repeat and chorus)
3: And the child chooses a cat . . . (repeat and chorus)

There is no direct translation of the words in the chorus.

Guide to pronunciation

staat	rhymes with *bat*
een (huis)	like the French *une*, but with a shorter *u*
huis	similar to *house*
daar	the *aa* is long, as in *aardvark*
woont	similar to *won't*
een (kind)	rhymes with *bun*
het	rhymes with *cut*, the *h* is almost silent
kind	rhymes with *wind*,
kiest	rhymes with *yeast*
een (kat)	rhymes with *bun*
ja	*yah*, rhymes with *car*
singela	the *g* is almost silent

THE CHANUKAH SONG

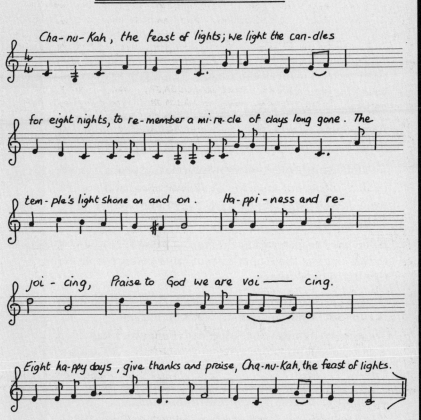

FURTHER READING

This play was based on Anne Frank's own writings, and Miep Gies' account of life in the annexe. You might like to read these books for yourself:

The Diary of Anne Frank, Anne Frank (Pan, 1968)
Anne Frank's Tales from the Secret Annexe (Penguin, 1986)
Anne Frank Remembered, Miep Gies (Corgi, 1988)

The following books give more information about Anne Frank:
In the Footsteps of Anne Frank, Ernst Schnabel (Pan, 1961)
Anne Frank in the World, Anne Frank Foundation (Bert Bakker, Amsterdam, 1985)

If you have been moved by the story of Anne Frank, you may like to read some of these novels about other young people living through difficult times:

Across the Barricades, Joan Lingard (Hamish Hamilton, 1972)
A story set in the troubles in Northern Ireland.

Walkabout, James Vance Marshall (Penguin, 1980)
A novel about prejudice and endurance in the Australian outback.

I am David, Anne Holm (Methuen, 1965)
A story that begins in a concentration camp.

The Silver Sword, Ian Serraillier (Jonathan Cape, 1956)
Polish children in the Second World War.

Z for Zachariah, Robert C O'Brien (Gollancz, 1977)
A story set after a nuclear war.

The Endless Steppe, Esther Hautzig (Heinemann, 1973)
A young Polish girl is sent to Siberia.

Words by Heart, Ouida Sebestyen (Collins Cascades, 1989)
A young black girl in the American South struggles against prejudice.